Introduction to *Daily Paragraph Editing*

Why *Daily Paragraph Editing?*

Daily Paragraph Editing is designed to help students master and retain grade-level skills in language mechanics and expression through focused, daily practice. Instead of practicing skills in a series of random, decontextualized exercises, *Daily Paragraph Editing* embeds language skills in paragraphs that represent the types of text that students encounter in their daily reading and writing activities across the curriculum. A weekly writing activity allows students to apply the skills they have been practicing throughout the week in their own short compositions.

What's in *Daily Paragraph Editing?*

Daily Paragraph Editing contains lessons for 36 weeks, with a separate lesson for each day.

Each week's lessons for Monday through Thursday consist of individual reproducible paragraphs that contain errors in the following skills:

- capitalization
- punctuation
- spelling
- language usage, and more

Student's daily lesson pages for Monday through Thursday include:

- a label indicating the type of writing modeled in the weekly lesson
- a paragraph with errors for students to correct; along with the other 3 paragraphs for the week, this forms a complete composition
- daily and weekly lesson identifiers
- as needed, the "Watch For" logo alerts students to more challenging skills to address in the paragraph

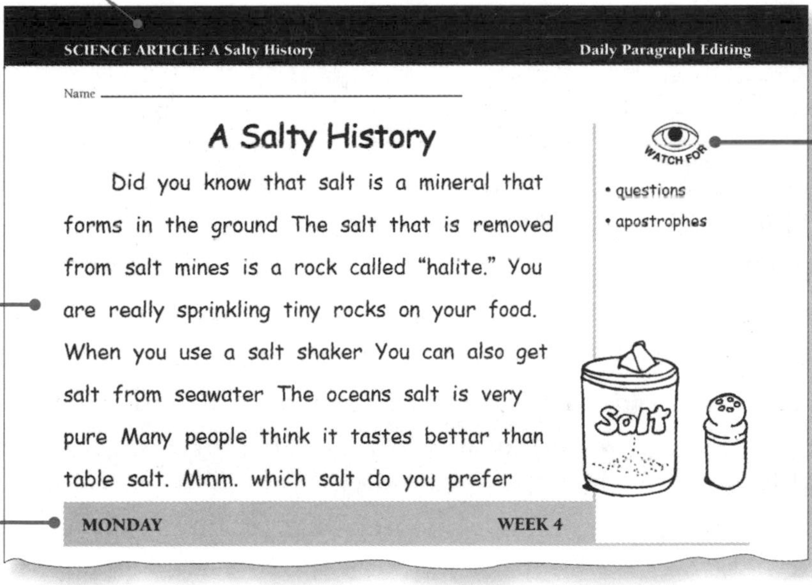

Students correct the errors in each daily paragraph by marking directly on the page. A reproducible sheet of Proofreading Marks (see page 10) helps familiarize students with the standard form for marking corrections on written text. Full-page Editing Keys show corrections for all errors in the daily paragraphs. Error Summaries help teachers identify the targeted skills in each week's lessons, and therefore help teachers plan to review or introduce the specific skills needed by their students.

Teacher's full-sized annotated Editing Key pages include:

- a label indicating the type of writing modeled in the weekly lesson
- the original student text with corrections marked in red (using the proofreading marks presented on page 10)
- daily and weekly lesson identifiers
- a summary of the errors in each paragraph to use in identifying unfamiliar skills to teach or review with students prior to assigning the paragraph. Some students may be more successful if you share the Error Summary with them before they read and edit the paragraph.

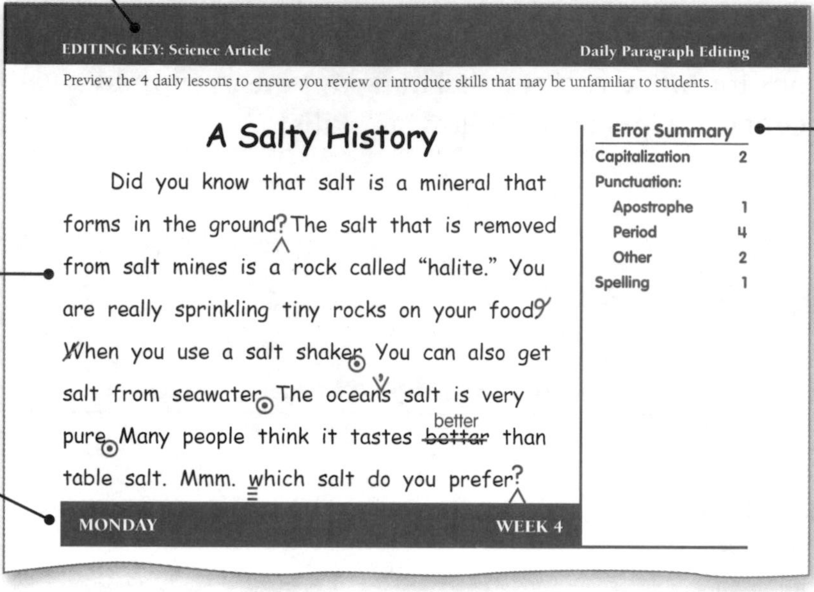
EDITING KEY: Science Article — Daily Paragraph Editing

Preview the 4 daily lessons to ensure you review or introduce skills that may be unfamiliar to students.

A Salty History

Did you know that salt is a mineral that forms in the ground? The salt that is removed from salt mines is a rock called "halite." You are really sprinkling tiny rocks on your food when you use a salt shaker. You can also get salt from seawater. The ocean's salt is very pure. Many people think it tastes better than table salt. Mmm. which salt do you prefer?

Error Summary	
Capitalization	2
Punctuation:	
Apostrophe	1
Period	4
Other	2
Spelling	1

MONDAY — WEEK 4

When corrected and read together, the four paragraphs for one week's lesson form a cohesive composition that also serves as a writing model for students. The weekly four-paragraph compositions cover a broad range of expository and narrative writing forms from across the curriculum, including the following:

- nonfiction texts on grade-level topics in social studies and science
- biographies, book reviews, editorials, instructions, interviews, journal entries, and letters
- fables, fantasy and science fiction, historical fiction, personal narratives, and realistic fiction

Each Friday lesson consists of a writing prompt that directs students to write in response to the week's four-paragraph composition. This gives students the opportunity to apply the skills they have practiced during the week in their own writing. Students gain experience writing in a wide variety of forms, always with the support of familiar models.

Friday writing prompts include:

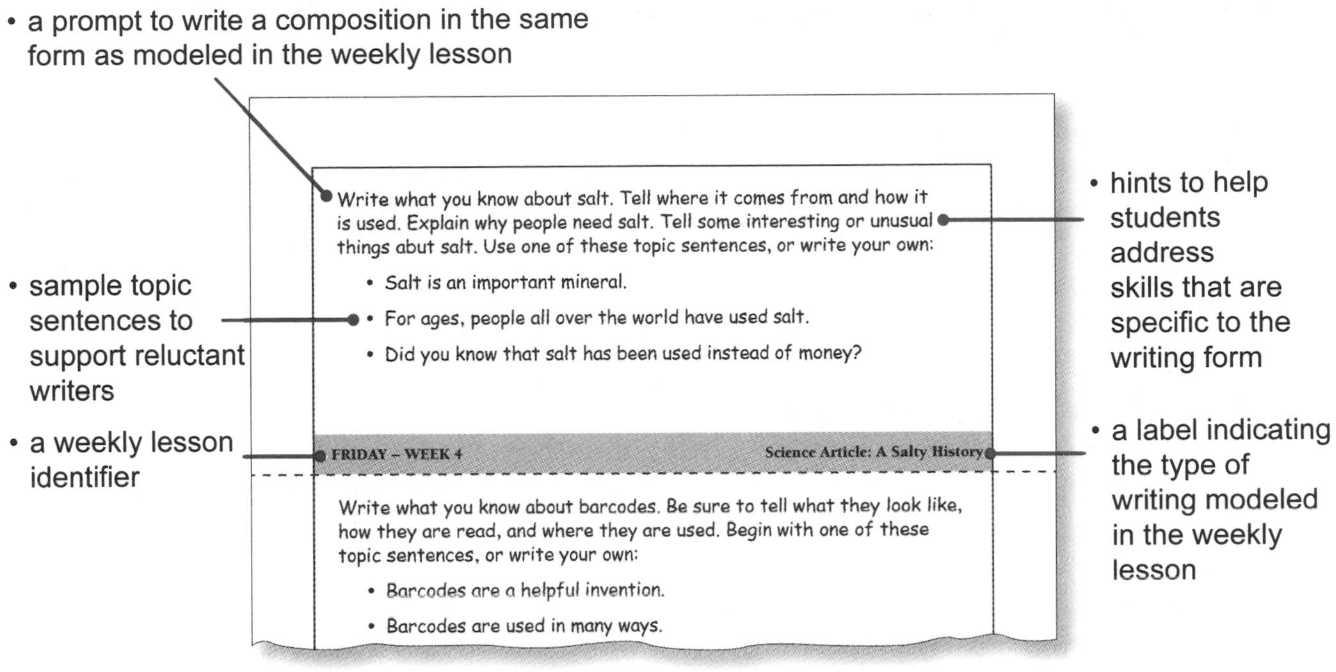

An Editing Checklist for students (see page 11) helps them revise their own writing or critique their peers' efforts. An Assessment Rubric (see page 9) is provided to help you assess student writing.

A reproducible student Language Handbook (pages 168–176) outlines the usage and mechanics rules for students to follow in editing the daily paragraphs. The Handbook includes examples to help familiarize students with how the conventions of language and mechanics are applied in authentic writing.

How to Use *Daily Paragraph Editing*

You may use *Daily Paragraph Editing* in several ways, depending on your instructional objectives and your students' needs. Over time, you will probably want to introduce each of the presentation strategies outlined below so you can identify the approach that works best for you and your students.

The four paragraphs that comprise each week's editing lessons include a set of errors that are repeated throughout all four paragraphs. We recommend that you provide a folder for students to keep their *Daily Paragraph Editing* reference materials and weekly lessons. It will work best to reproduce and distribute all four daily paragraphs for a given week on Monday. That way, students can use the previous days' lessons for reference as the week progresses.

Directed Group Lessons

Daily Paragraph Editing activities will be most successful if you first introduce them as a group activity. You might also have students edit individual copies of the day's lesson as you work through the paragraph with the group. Continue presenting the Monday through Thursday lessons to the entire class until you are confident that students are familiar with the editing process. Try any of the following methods to direct group lessons:

Option 1

1. Create and display an overhead transparency of the day's paragraph.
2. Read the paragraph aloud just as it is written, including all the errors.
3. Read the paragraph a second time, using phrasing and intonation that would be appropriate if all end punctuation were correct. (You may find it helpful to read from the Editing Key.) Read all other errors as they appear in the text.
4. Guide students in correcting all end punctuation and initial capitals in the paragraph; mark corrections in erasable pen on the overhead transparency.
5. After the paragraph is correctly divided into sentences, review it one sentence at a time. Have volunteers point out errors as you come to them, and identify the necessary corrections. Encourage students to explain the reason for each correction; explain or clarify any rules that are unfamiliar.

Option 2

Follow Steps 1–4 on page 4, and then work with students to focus on one type of error at a time, correcting all errors of the same type (i.e., capitalization, commas, subject/verb agreement, spelling, etc.) in the paragraph before moving on to another type. Refer to the Error Summary in the Editing Key to help you identify the various types of errors.

Option 3

Use directed group lesson time to conduct a minilesson on one or more of the skills emphasized in that day's lesson. This is especially appropriate for new or unfamiliar skills, or for skills that are especially challenging or confusing for students. After introducing a specific skill, use the approach outlined in Option 2 to focus on that skill in one or more of the week's daily paragraphs. To provide additional practice, refer to the Skills Scope & Sequence to find other paragraphs that include the same target skill.

Individual Practice

Once students are familiar with the process for editing the daily paragraphs, they may work on their own or with a partner to make corrections. Be sure students have their Proofreading Marks available to help them mark their corrections. Remind students to refer to the student Language Handbook as needed for guidance in the rules of mechanics and usage. Some students may find it helpful to know at the outset the number and types of errors they are seeking. Provide this information by referring to the Error Summary on the annotated Editing Key pages. You may wish to use a transparency on the overhead to check work with the group. Occasionally, you may wish to assess students' acquisition of skills by collecting and reviewing their work before they check it.

Customizing Instruction

Some of the skills covered in *Daily Paragraph Editing* may not be part of the grade-level expectancies in the language program you use. Some skills may even be taught differently in your program from the way they are modeled in *Daily Paragraph Editing*. In such cases, follow the approach used in your program. Simply revise the paragraph text as needed by covering it with correction fluid or by writing in changes before you reproduce copies for students.

Comma usage is an area where discrepancies are most likely to arise. *Daily Paragraph Editing* uses the "closed" style, where commas are included after short introductory phrases. Except for commas used in salutations, closings, dates, and between city and state in letters, journals, or news articles, all commas that appear in the daily paragraphs have been correctly placed according to the closed style. All other skills related to the use of commas are practiced by requiring students to insert missing commas, rather than moving or deleting extraneous commas.

Occasionally, you or your students may make a correction that differs from that shown in the Editing Key. The decision to use an exclamation mark instead of a period, or a period instead of a semicolon, is often a subjective decision made by individual writers. When discrepancies of this sort arise, capitalize on the "teachable moment" to let students know that there are gray areas in English usage and mechanics, and discuss how each of the possible correct choices can affect the meaning or tone of the writing.

You may wish to have your students mark corrections on the daily paragraphs in a manner that differs from the common proofreading marks on page 10. If so, model the marking style you wish students to follow as you conduct group lessons on an overhead, and point out any differences between the standard proofing marks and those to be used by your students.

Using the Writing Prompts

Have students keep their daily paragraphs in a folder so they can review the week's four corrected paragraphs on Friday. Identify the type of writing modeled in the four-paragraph composition and any of its special features (e.g., dialog in a fictional narrative; salutation, closing, and paragraph style in a letter; opinion statements and supporting arguments in an editorial; etc.).

Present the Friday writing prompt on an overhead transparency, write it on the board, or distribute individual copies to students. Take a few minutes to brainstorm ideas with the group and to focus on language skills that students will need to address in their writing.

After students complete their writing, encourage them to use the Editing Checklist (see page 11) to review or revise their work. You may also wish to have partners review each other's writing. To conduct a more formal assessment of students' writing, use the Assessment Rubric on page 9.

If you assign paragraph writing for homework, be sure students have the week's four corrected paragraphs available as a reference. You may wish to set aside some time for volunteers to read their completed writing to the class, or display compositions on a weekly writing bulletin board for students to enjoy.

Skills Scope and Sequence

Week No.

Capitalization	1	2	3	4	5	6	7	8	9	10	11	12	13	14	15	16	17	18	19	20	21	22	23	24	25	26	27	28	29	30	31	32	33	34	35	36
Beginning of Sentences, Quotations, Salutations/Closings	●	●				●		●	●		●	●		●	●	●	●	●	●	●	●	●	●				●	●	●	●	●	●	●		●	●
Days & Months		●	●			●	●	●		●	●	●				●	●			●							●	●	●					●		●
Holidays											●																		●							●
Incorrect Use of Capitals	●		●	●					●	●								●			●			●			●				●		●		●	●
Names & Titles of People, incl. Languages, Nationalities	●	●	●				●		●	●		●	●			●	●	●					●	●			●	●			●					●
Names of Places, Historic Events			●			●	●			●		●	●			●				●				●		●	●				●			●		
Nouns Used as Names (Aunt, Grandpa, etc.)								●						●													●							●		
Titles of Books, Magazines, Poems, Stories			●						●		●					●		●				●														●
Titles of Movies, TV Shows, Songs											●								●	●																
Word *I*			●											●			●												●							

Language Usage	1	2	3	4	5	6	7	8	9	10	11	12	13	14	15	16	17	18	19	20	21	22	23	24	25	26	27	28	29	30	31	32	33	34	35	36
Correct Use of Singular & Plural Forms					●						●				●					●					●		●				●					
Correct Use of Verb Tenses	●														●										●											
Use of Correct Adjective & Adverbial Forms																					●												●		●	
Use of Correct Pronouns																											●	●								

Punctuation: Apostrophes	1	2	3	4	5	6	7	8	9	10	11	12	13	14	15	16	17	18	19	20	21	22	23	24	25	26	27	28	29	30	31	32	33	34	35	36
In Contractions							●	●	●	●				●				●	●	●	●	●	●		●	●		●	●	●	●			●		
In Possessives	●			●				●					●			●	●			●		●					●				●	●	●	●		
Improperly Placed				●									●			●		●																	●	

Punctuation: Commas	1	2	3	4	5	6	7	8	9	10	11	12	13	14	15	16	17	18	19	20	21	22	23	24	25	26	27	28	29	30	31	32	33	34	35	36
After Introductory Dependent Phrase or Clause																																●	●			
After Introductory Interjection or Expression							●		●																											
After Salutation & Closing in a Letter			●					●																●					●							
Between City & State & City & Country Names			●				●			●	●									●				●												
Between Equally Modifying Adjectives						●								●		●								●				●							●	
Between Items in a Series				●	●		●	●	●													●	●			●	●		●	●						
In a Date		●	●				●	●			●	●																	●					●		
To Separate Parts of Compound Sentences	●								●				●							●	●	●		●							●		●	●	●	●
To Set Off Appositives			●						●				●				●											●								
To Set Off Quotations							●	●									●		●				●		●			●						●		
With Name Used in Direct Address																	●		●															●		

Skills Scope and Sequence (continued)

	Week No.																																			
Punctuation: Periods	1	2	3	4	5	6	7	8	9	10	11	12	13	14	15	16	17	18	19	20	21	22	23	24	25	26	27	28	29	30	31	32	33	34	35	36
After Initials		•					•		•				•		•					•		•														
At End of Sentence	•	•	•	•	•	•		•	•	•	•	•		•	•			•	•	•	•	•	•	•	•	•	•	•	•	•	•	•	•	•	•	•
In Address Abbreviations			•																					•												
In Time & Measurement Abbreviations			•			•													•	•	•												•		•	•
In Title Abbreviations			•				•			•										•		•														
To Correct Run-on & Rambling Sentences; Fragments				•																	•						•				•		•		•	
Punctuation: Quotation Marks	1	2	3	4	5	6	7	8	9	10	11	12	13	14	15	16	17	18	19	20	21	22	23	24	25	26	27	28	29	30	31	32	33	34	35	36
In Speech							•	•									•		•	•					•			•						•		
With Titles of Works of Art, Articles, Poems, Chapters, Short Stories, Songs, Newspaper Articles	•		•								•					•			•	•		•														
Improper Placement									•		•					•	•		•					•				•								
Punctuation: Other	1	2	3	4	5	6	7	8	9	10	11	12	13	14	15	16	17	18	19	20	21	22	23	24	25	26	27	28	29	30	31	32	33	34	35	36
Colon in Time								•											•																	•
Exclamation Point				•			•	•										•	•	•			•		•			•		•						
Hyphen in Fractions																•								•		•										
Periods & Commas Inside Quotation Marks				•																			•													
Question Mark		•		•	•				•	•	•				•		•	•										•		•		•				
Underline Names of Aircraft & Ships										•	•	•	•											•												
Underline Titles of Books, Magazines, Movies, Newspapers, TV Shows	•		•						•		•					•		•	•			•														•
Spelling	1	2	3	4	5	6	7	8	9	10	11	12	13	14	15	16	17	18	19	20	21	22	23	24	25	26	27	28	29	30	31	32	33	34	35	36
Identify Errors in Grade-Level Words	•	•	•	•	•	•	•	•	•		•	•	•	•	•	•	•	•	•	•	•	•	•	•	•	•	•	•	•	•	•	•	•	•	•	•

Assessment Rubric for Evaluating Friday Paragraph Writing

The Friday writing prompts give students the opportunity to use the capitalization, punctuation, and other usage and mechanics skills that have been practiced during the week's editing tasks. They also require students to write in a variety of different forms and genres.

In evaluating students' Friday paragraphs, you may wish to focus exclusively on their mastery of the aspects of mechanics and usage targeted that week. However, if you wish to conduct a more global assessment of student writing, the following rubric offers broad guidelines for evaluating the composition as a whole.

Characteristics of Student Writing

	EXCELLENT	GOOD	FAIR	WEAK
Clarity and Focus	Writing is exceptionally clear, focused, and interesting.	Writing is generally clear, focused, and interesting.	Writing is loosely focused on the topic.	Writing is unclear and unfocused.
Development of Main Ideas	Main ideas are clear, specific, and well-developed.	Main ideas are identifiable, but may be somewhat general.	Main ideas are overly broad or simplistic.	Main ideas are unclear or not expressed.
Organization	Organization is clear (beginning, middle, and end) and fits the topic and writing form.	Organization is clear, but may be predictable or formulaic.	Organization is attempted, but is often unclear.	Organization is not coherent.
Use of Details	Details are relevant, specific, and well-placed.	Details are relevant, but may be overly general.	Details may be off-topic, predictable, or not specific enough.	Details are absent or insufficient to support main ideas.
Vocabulary	Vocabulary is exceptionally rich, varied, and well-chosen.	Vocabulary is colorful and generally avoids clichés.	Vocabulary is ordinary and may rely on clichés.	Vocabulary is limited, general, or vague.
Mechanics and Usage	Demonstrates exceptionally strong command of conventions of punctuation, capitalization, spelling, and usage.	Demonstrates control of conventions of punctuation, capitalization, spelling, and usage.	Errors in use of conventions of mechanics and usage distract, but do not impede, the reader.	Limited ability to control conventions of mechanics and usage impairs readability of the composition.

Proofreading Marks

Use these marks to show corrections.

Mark	Meaning	Example
℘	Take this out (delete).	I love ~~to~~ to read.
⊙	Add a period.	It was late⊙
≡	Make this a capital letter.	First prize went to maria. (≡ under m)
/	Make this a lowercase letter.	We saw a /Black /Cat.
——	Fix the spelling.	This is our ~~hause~~ house.
^,	Add a comma.	Goodnight^, Mom.
∨'	Add an apostrophe.	It∨'s mine.
∨" ∨"	Add quotation marks.	∨"Come in,∨" he said.
^! ^?	Add an exclamation point or a question mark.	Help^! Can you help me^?
^-	Add a hyphen.	I've read three^-fourths of the book.
⁀ ‿	Close the space.	Foot⁀‿ball is fun.
^	Add a word.	The ^red pen is mine.
——	Underline the words.	We read <u>Old Yeller</u>.
^:	Add a colon.	Alex arrived at 4^:00.

Editing Checklist

Use this checklist to review and revise your writing:

○ Does each sentence begin with a capital letter?
○ Do names of people and places begin with a capital letter?
○ Does each sentence end with a period, a question mark, or an exclamation point?
○ Did I use apostrophes to show possession (*Ana's desk*) and in contractions (*isn't*)?
○ Did I choose the correct word (*to, too, two*)?
○ Did I check for spelling errors?
○ Did I place commas where they are needed?
○ Are my sentences clear and complete?

Editing Checklist

Use this checklist to review and revise your writing:

○ Does each sentence begin with a capital letter?
○ Do names of people and places begin with a capital letter?
○ Does each sentence end with a period, a question mark, or an exclamation point?
○ Did I use apostrophes to show possession (*Ana's desk*) and in contractions (*isn't*)?
○ Did I choose the correct word (*to, too, two*)?
○ Did I check for spelling errors?
○ Did I place commas where they are needed?
○ Are my sentences clear and complete?

©2004 by Evan-Moor Corp. • Daily Paragraph Editing • EMC 2726

Preview the 4 daily lessons to ensure you review or introduce skills that may be unfamiliar to students.

Walt Disney's Cartoon Magic

Walt Disney lived on a farm when he was a young boy. From an early age, walt liked to draw animals. He watched the farm animals carefully he made lifelike drawings of them. Walts family had no money for paper but Walt was clever. he drawed (drew) a pig on the wall of his house. Walt's parents were not happy! Then Walts aunt gave him drawing paper

Error Summary	
Capitalization	3
Language Usage	1
Punctuation:	
Apostrophe	2
Comma	1
Period	2

MONDAY WEEK 1

When walt grew up, he got a job drawing animuls (animals) for animated cartoons. creative ideas filled Walts head. the other cartoons were silent so Walt made a cartoon with music and talking characters. This cartoon was called <u>Steamboat Willie</u>. The star was mickey Mouse. Mickey talked and singed (sang) people loved him

Error Summary	
Capitalization	5
Language Usage	1
Punctuation:	
Apostrophe	1
Comma	1
Period	2
Spelling	1

TUESDAY WEEK 1

Name ______________________________

Walt Disney's Cartoon Magic

Walt Disney lived on a farm when he was a young boy. From an early age, walt liked to draw animals. He watched the farm animals carefully he made lifelike drawings of them. Walts family had no money for paper but Walt was clever. he drawed a pig on the wall of his house. Walt's parents were not happy! Then Walts aunt gave him drawing paper

WATCH FOR

• apostrophes

MONDAY **WEEK 1**

When walt grew up, he got a job drawing animuls for animated cartoons. creative ideas filled Walts head. the other cartoons were silent so Walt made a cartoon with music and talking characters. This cartoon was called <u>Steamboat Willie</u>. The star was mickey Mouse. Mickey talked and singed, people loved him

WATCH FOR

• apostrophes

TUESDAY **WEEK 1**

Walt liked to try new things. most cartoons were only a few minutes long. Walt wanted to make a two-hour animated film. some ~~peopil~~ people said it was a bad idea but Walt believed in himself He made Snow White and the Seven Dwarfs. The Audience cheered at the end. as they ~~leaved~~ left the theater, they hummed "Whistle While You Work.

Error Summary	
Capitalization	4
Language Usage	1
Punctuation:	
Comma	1
Period	1
Quotation Mark	1
Other	1
Spelling	1

WEDNESDAY WEEK 1

Disney's new ideas changed animated films forever He was full of energy and over the years ~~maked~~ made many popular cartoon films. People have been watching Peter Pan, Bambi, and other disney films for years. people will watch them ~~fer~~ for years to come. they'll keep singing songs like When You Wish Upon a Star.

Error Summary	
Capitalization	3
Language Usage	1
Punctuation:	
Period	1
Quotation Mark	2
Other	2
Spelling	1

THURSDAY WEEK 1

Name ______________________________

Walt liked to try new things. most cartoons were only a few minutes long. Walt wanted to make a two-hour animated film. some peopil said it was a bad idea but Walt believed in himself He made Snow White and the Seven Dwarfs. The Audience cheered at the end. as they leaved the theater, they hummed “Whistle While You Work.

WATCH FOR

- titles of movies and songs

WEDNESDAY **WEEK 1**

Disney's new ideas changed animated films forever He was full of energy and over the years maked many popular cartoon films. People have been watching Peter Pan, Bambi, and other disney films for years. people will watch them fer years to come. they'll keep singing songs like When You Wish Upon a Star.

WATCH FOR

- titles of movies and songs

THURSDAY **WEEK 1**

Preview the 4 daily lessons to ensure you review or introduce skills that may be unfamiliar to students.

The Search for Planets

Planets are large objects in space⊙ they travel around the sun. In earlier times, people thought there were six planets⊙They knew about Earth, mars, and venus. They knew about mercury, jupiter, and saturn. Was anything else out there? Early telescopes were too weak to spot other planets⊙

Error Summary

Capitalization	6
Punctuation:	
Period	3
Other	1

MONDAY WEEK 2

march 13, 1781, was an important day. F. william herschel and caroline L⊙herschel discovered a seventh planet⊙ they called it uranus⊙They wondered if there were still more planets out in space⊙Some people thought so. They kept looking because they were curious⊙

Error Summary

Capitalization	7
Punctuation:	
Comma	1
Period	5

TUESDAY WEEK 2

Name ______________________________

The Search for Planets

Planets are large objects in space they travel around the sun. In earlier times, people thought there were six planets They knew about Earth, mars, and venus. They knew about mercury, jupiter, and saturn. Was anything else out there Early telescopes were too weak to spot other planets

WATCH FOR

- names of planets
- questions

MONDAY **WEEK 2**

march 13 1781, was an important day. F. william herschel and caroline L herschel discovered a seventh planet they called it uranus They wondered if there were still more planets out in space Some people thought so. They kept looking because they were curious

WATCH FOR

- names of people and planets

TUESDAY **WEEK 2**

jean J. Le Verrier thought he knew where another planet was. he asked johanne G. galle and heinrich L. d'Arrest to look for it. That very night, they thought they saw something. What was it? By the next night, they ~~new~~ knew that it was a ~~planett~~ planet. Thanks to their work, neptune became the eighth known planet on september 24, 1846.

Error Summary	
Capitalization	7
Punctuation:	
Comma	1
Period	4
Other	1
Spelling	2

WEDNESDAY **WEEK 2**

What was beyond neptune? Dr. clyde W. tombaugh found out. He discovered pluto on february 18, 1930. It became the ninth known planet. If all ~~gose~~ goes well, a spacecraft will fly past pluto in 2016. It will take pictures. the pictures should tell us a lot. Are there more planets beyond pluto? What do you think?

Error Summary	
Capitalization	8
Punctuation:	
Comma	1
Period	2
Other	3
Spelling	1

THURSDAY **WEEK 2**

Name ______________________________

jean J. Le Verrier thought he knew where another planet was he asked johanne G galle and heinrich L d'Arrest to look for it. That very night, they thought they saw something. What was it By the next night, they new that it was a planett. Thanks to their work, neptune became the eighth known planet on september 24 1846

WATCH FOR

- names of people and planets
- questions

WEDNESDAY **WEEK 2**

What was beyond neptune Dr. clyde W tombaugh found out. He discovered pluto on february 18 1930. It became the ninth known planet. If all gose well, a spacecraft will fly past pluto in 2016. It will take pictures the pictures should tell us a lot. Are there more planets beyond pluto What do you think

WATCH FOR

- names of people and planets
- questions

THURSDAY **WEEK 2**

Preview the 4 daily lessons to ensure you review or introduce skills that may be unfamiliar to students.

Letters to an Author

604 W tabb lakes Dr

yorktown VA 23693

february 24 2004

Dear Mrs faith ringgold

My name is sara, and I am in the third grade Our teacher, ms. brock read Tar Beach to us. i likied it a lot

liked

Error Summary	
Capitalization	10
Punctuation:	
Comma	4
Period	5
Other	1
Spelling	1

MONDAY WEEK 3

Ms; brock said that your drawings are story quilts that you painted. I like the way they look in tar beach i read Cassie's Word Quilt to my little sister, erma. I can't wait to read the rest of your books

Sincerely

sara T sanchez

Error Summary	
Capitalization	7
Punctuation:	
Comma	1
Period	4
Other	2

TUESDAY WEEK 3

Name ______________________________

Letters to an Author

604 W tabb lakes Dr

yorktown VA 23693

february 24. 2004

Dear Mrs faith ringgold

My name is sara, and I am in the third grade Our teacher, ms. brock read Tar Beach to us. i likied it a lot

WATCH FOR

- address
- commas
- book titles

MONDAY **WEEK 3**

Ms: brock said that your drawings are story quilts that you painted. I like the way they look in tar beach i read Cassie's Word Quilt to my little sister, erma. I can't wait to read the rest of your books

Sincerely

sara T sanchez

WATCH FOR

- commas
- book titles

TUESDAY **WEEK 3**

813 E cactus St
portland TX 78374
may 7 2004

Dear Mrs faith ringgold;
i found your song, "Anyone Can Fly, on
your Web site My teacher Mr cohen, let me
teech (teach) it to the class

Error Summary	
Capitalization	7
Punctuation:	
Comma	4
Period	6
Quotation Mark	1
Spelling	1

WEDNESDAY WEEK 3

Everyone in the class liked "anyone can fly."
i hope You write more songs mr. cohen is now
reading The Invisible Princess to us. The story
quilt drawings are wunderful (wonderful). Next, i am going
to read bonjour, lonnie

Your fan
lakeesha R wilson

Error Summary	
Capitalization	12
Punctuation:	
Comma	1
Period	3
Other	2
Spelling	1

THURSDAY WEEK 3

Name ______________________________

813 E cactus St

portland TX 78374

may 7: 2004

Dear Mrs faith ringgold;

i found your song, “Anyone Can Fly, on your Web site My teacher Mr cohen, let me teech it to the class

WATCH FOR

- address
- commas
- song titles

WEDNESDAY **WEEK 3**

Everyone in the class liked “anyone can fly.” i hope You write more songs mr. cohen is now reading The Invisible Princess to us. The story quilt drawings are wunderful. Next, i am going to read bonjour, lonnie

Your fan

lakeesha R wilson

WATCH FOR

- commas
- book and song titles

THURSDAY **WEEK 3**

Preview the 4 daily lessons to ensure you review or introduce skills that may be unfamiliar to students.

A Salty History

Did you know that salt is a mineral that forms in the ground? The salt that is removed from salt mines is a rock called "halite." You are really sprinkling tiny rocks on your food when you use a salt shaker. You can also get salt from seawater. The ocean's salt is very pure. Many people think it tastes better than table salt. Mmm. Which salt do you prefer?

Error Summary	
Capitalization	2
Punctuation:	
Apostrophe	1
Period	4
Other	2
Spelling	1

MONDAY WEEK 4

Do we need salt? Yes, we do. Our cells need salt to stay alive. As a matter of fact, salt makes up nearly one percent of our body's blood and cells. Salt is used to preserve foods because it kills germs. Salt is also used to make glass, soap, and other items. One kind of salt is used in popular ice-cream machines.

Error Summary	
Capitalization	2
Punctuation:	
Apostrophe	1
Comma	1
Period	1
Other	1
Spelling	1

TUESDAY WEEK 4

Name ____________________

A Salty History

Did you know that salt is a mineral that forms in the ground The salt that is removed from salt mines is a rock called "halite." You are really sprinkling tiny rocks on your food. When you use a salt shaker You can also get salt from seawater The oceans salt is very pure Many people think it tastes bettar than table salt. Mmm. which salt do you prefer

WATCH FOR

- questions
- apostrophes

MONDAY **WEEK 4**

Do we need salt Yes, we do. Our cells need salt to stay alife. As a matter of fact, salt makes up nearly one percent of our bodys blood and cells. Salt is used to preserve foods because it kills germs salt is also used to make glass soap, and other items. one kind of salt is used in popular ice-cream machines.

WATCH FOR

- questions
- apostrophes

TUESDAY **WEEK 4**

Polands famous salt mines are very ~~inusual~~ unusual. For hundreds of years, miners have dug salt from deep beneath the Earths' surface. They have carved elegant rooms and beautiful statues from the solid salt curious tourists visit to see the miners statues. wow! would you like to see them?

Error Summary	
Capitalization	3
Punctuation:	
Apostrophe	3
Period	1
Other	2
Spelling	1

WEDNESDAY **WEEK 4**

Across the ages and ~~arownd~~ around the world, salt has been valued very highly it was important and hard to obtain. The ancient Roman soldiers' wages were paid in salt Their word for "salt" was "sal" That is where our word "salary" come's from. Gee, would you like to get paid in salt? In many places, salt is still a symbol of friendship

Error Summary	
Capitalization	1
Punctuation:	
Period	4
Other	1
Spelling	2

THURSDAY **WEEK 4**

Name ____________________________________

Polands famous salt mines are very inusual. For hundreds of years, miners have dug salt from deep beneath the Earths' surface. They have carved elegant rooms and beautiful statues from the solid salt curious tourists visit to see the miners statues. wow would you like to see them

WATCH FOR

- questions
- apostrophes

WEDNESDAY **WEEK 4**

Across the ages and arownd the world, salt has been valued very highly it was important and hard to obtain. The ancient Roman soldiers' wages were paid in salt Their word for "salt" was "sal" That is where our word "salary" come's from. Gee, would you like to get paid in salt In many places, salt is still a symbol of friendship

WATCH FOR

- questions
- apostrophes

THURSDAY **WEEK 4**

Preview the 4 daily lessons to ensure you review or introduce skills that may be unfamiliar to students.

Barcodes

What is a barcode? Look on the bottom of a cereal box. Do you see a group of black bars and spaces? That's a barcode. A barcode identifies a product. The thin bars, thick bars, and white ~~spases~~ spaces are used in a different way for each product.

Error Summary

Punctuation:	
Comma	2
Period	2
Other	2
Spelling	1

MONDAY **WEEK 5**

Where are barcodes used? The first barcodes were used in supermarkets. Clothing, toy, book, and other stores also use them now. the barcodes help stores keep track of what they sell. ~~Eech~~ Each item in a library has a barcode. The post office uses barcodes to track mail.

Error Summary

Capitalization	1
Punctuation:	
Comma	3
Period	1
Other	1
Spelling	1

TUESDAY **WEEK 5**

Name ________________________________

Barcodes

What is a barcode Look on the bottom of a cereal box. Do you see a group of black bars and spaces That's a barcode A barcode identifies a product. The thin bars thick bars and white spases are used in a different way for each product

WATCH FOR
- questions
- commas

MONDAY **WEEK 5**

Where are barcodes used The first barcodes were used in supermarkets. Clothing toy book and other stores also use them now. the barcodes help stores keep track of what they sell. Eech item in a library has a barcode. The post office uses barcodes to track mail

WATCH FOR
- questions
- commas

TUESDAY **WEEK 5**

How is a barcode read? A barcode reader reads the code. A laser beam in the reader ~~reeds~~ reads the pattern of thin lines, thick lines, and spaces. It translates the pattern into numbers. The numbers are sent to a computer. The computer stores the information.

Error Summary

Punctuation:

Comma	2
Period	2
Other	1
Spelling	1

WEDNESDAY **WEEK 5**

Can barcodes be used with people or animals? Yes. Barcodes are used in hospitals, blood banks, and offices. Hospital barcodes have facts about the patients. Blood banks use barcodes to label the ~~bludd~~ blood. Some companies use barcode ID cards for their workers. Researchers put barcodes on animals.

Error Summary

Punctuation:

Comma	2
Period	1
Other	1
Spelling	1

THURSDAY **WEEK 5**

Name ____

How is a barcode read A barcode reader reads the code A laser beam in the reader reeds the pattern of thin lines thick lines and spaces. It translates the pattern into numbers. The numbers are sent to a computer. The computer stores the information

WATCH FOR

- questions
- commas

WEDNESDAY **WEEK 5**

Can barcodes be used with people or animals Yes. Barcodes are used in hospitals blood banks and offices. Hospital barcodes have facts about the patients. Blood banks use barcodes to label the bludd. Some companies use barcode ID cards for their workers. Researchers put barcodes on animals

WATCH FOR

- questions
- commas

THURSDAY **WEEK 5**

Preview the 4 daily lessons to ensure you review or introduce skills that may be unfamiliar to students.

The Grand Canyon

The Grand Canyon is a long deep cut in the land. it is about 448 kilometers (278 mi) long It goes across northern arizona. stand allong the wide flat rim Look down into a vast rugged wilderness see rocks that are millions of years old. the layers of rock look like colorful striped pancakes

along

Error Summary	
Capitalization	5
Punctuation:	
Comma	4
Period	5
Spelling	1

MONDAY **WEEK 6**

some parts of the grand canyon have steep rocky slopes There are no trees or plants. Othar parts have short stubby bushes. columns of rock up to a mile (5,280 ft) high reach up from the canyon floor The Vulcan's Throne is a volcano cone. it rises 172 meters (567 f t) from a rock shelf

Other

Error Summary	
Capitalization	5
Punctuation:	
Comma	2
Period	5
Spelling	1

TUESDAY **WEEK 6**

Name ______________________________

The Grand Canyon

The Grand Canyon is a long deep cut in the land. it is about 448 kilometers (278 mi) long It goes across northern arizona. stand allong the wide flat rim Look down into a vast rugged wilderness see rocks that are millions of years old. the layers of rock look like colorful striped pancakes

WATCH FOR

- commas
- abbreviations

MONDAY **WEEK 6**

some parts of the grand canyon have steep rocky slopes There are no trees or plants. Othar parts have short stubby bushes. columns of rock up to a mile (5,280 ft) high reach up from the canyon floor The Vulcan's Throne is a volcano cone. it rises 172 meters (567 f.t) from a rock shelf

WATCH FOR

- commas
- abbreviations

TUESDAY **WEEK 6**

The northern rim is the coolest, wettest part of the Grand canyon. it has harsh, freezing winters. The coldest month is january. There may be up to 130 inches (11 f.t.) of snow on the ground. the ~~hotest~~ hottest month is july. less than 15 centimeters (6 in.) of rain fall during the hot, dry summer.

Error Summary

Capitalization	6
Punctuation:	
Comma	4
Period	6
Spelling	1

WEDNESDAY **WEEK 6**

The colorado river flows along the bottom of the Grand canyon. it looks like a slick, winding ribbon! most of the river is about 15 meters (50 ft.) deep. After a rain, the river is a muddy, reddish-brown ~~kolor~~ color. the river has about 40 kilometers (25 m.i.) of swift, foaming rapids. The rest of the river flows at a calm, slow pace.

Error Summary

Capitalization	6
Punctuation:	
Comma	4
Period	5
Spelling	1

THURSDAY **WEEK 6**

Name ______________________________

The northern rim is the coolest wettest part of the Grand canyon. it has harsh freezing winters The coldest month is january There may be up to 130 inches (11 f,t,) of snow on the ground the hotest month is july. less than 15 centimeters (6 in) of rain fall during the hot dry summer

WATCH FOR

- commas
- abbreviations

WEDNESDAY **WEEK 6**

The colorado river flows along the bottom of the Grand canyon. it looks like a slick winding ribbon! most of the river is about 15 meters (50 ft,) deep After a rain, the river is a muddy reddish-brown kolor. the river has about 40 kilometers (25 m.i.) of swift foaming rapids The rest of the river flows at a calm slow pace

WATCH FOR

- commas
- abbreviations

THURSDAY **WEEK 6**

Preview the 4 daily lessons to ensure you review or introduce skills that may be unfamiliar to students.

News on the Wing

Butterflies Return to mexico

february 21 2003

There's a forest near mexico city mexico. Why are the trees black and ~~oranje~~ orange? Its the wings of 500 million monarch ~~butterflys~~ butterflies. Scientists tourists and locals are thrilled. mrs elva m cruz said Oh theyre so pretty! They come in october and leave in march."

Error Summary	
Capitalization	11
Punctuation:	
Apostrophe	3
Comma	6
Period	2
Quotation Mark	1
Spelling	2

MONDAY WEEK 7

january 2002 was a tough month in mexico. There was hard ~~rane~~ rain frost and very cold weather. Sadly, three-fourths of the butterflies died. dr juan r campa said, Some of them lived. We didnt know what would happen to them. Luckily, they flew to texas florida and other states. Their offspring have now come back."

Error Summary	
Capitalization	8
Punctuation:	
Apostrophe	1
Comma	4
Period	2
Quotation Mark	1
Spelling	1

TUESDAY WEEK 7

Name ______________________________

News on the Wing

Butterflies Return to mexico

february 21 2003

Theres a forest near mexico city mexico. Why are the trees black and oranje? Its the wings of 500 million monarch butterflys. Scientists tourists and locals are thrilled. mrs elva m cruz said Oh theyre so pretty! They come in october and leave in march."

WATCH FOR

- names of people and places
- commas
- dialog

MONDAY **WEEK 7**

january 2002 was a tough month in mexico. There was hard rane frost and very cold weather. Sadly, three-fourths of the butterflies died. dr juan r campa said, Some of them lived. We didnt know what would happen to them. Luckily, they flew to texas florida and other states. Their offspring have now come back."

WATCH FOR

- names of people and places
- commas
- dialog

TUESDAY **WEEK 7**

Robins Flock to virginia

february 23, 2003

Usually, virginia has some robins. This february, there are millions more. dr. greg k. Hill said, "Many of these birds are from states like georgia. They go to new jersey, new york, and other northern states for the ~~sumer~~ summer. They'll stop in virginia, and then fly on."

Error Summary

Capitalization	13
Punctuation:	
Apostrophe	1
Comma	4
Period	2
Quotation Mark	2
Spelling	1

WEDNESDAY WEEK 7

dr. hill also said that december, january, and february were very cold. The ground in the Northeast is still frozen. The birds can't find worms, insects, or any other food there. They're staying in virginia ~~insted~~ instead of flying north. Folks in richmond, yorktown, and norfolk are happy. mrs. b. k. marks said, "Wow! I love their singing."

Error Summary

Capitalization	13
Punctuation:	
Apostrophe	2
Comma	7
Period	4
Quotation Mark	2
Other	1
Spelling	1

THURSDAY WEEK 7

Name ______________________________

Robins Flock to virginia

february 23 2003

Usually, virginia has some robins. This february, there are millions more. dr greg k Hill said Many of these birds are from states like georgia. They go to new jersey new york and other northern states for the sumer. Theyll stop in virginia, and then fly on.

WATCH FOR

- names of people and places
- commas
- dialog

WEDNESDAY　　**WEEK 7**

dr hill also said that december january and february were very cold. The ground in the Northeast is still frozen. The birds cant find worms insects or any other food there. Theyre staying in virginia instedd of flying north. Folks in richmond yorktown and norfolk are happy. mrs b k marks said Wow I love their singing.

WATCH FOR

- names of people and places
- commas
- dialog

THURSDAY　　**WEEK 7**

Preview the 4 daily lessons to ensure you review or introduce skills that may be unfamiliar to students.

Rosie's Diary

wednesday june 9 2004

dear diary

On tuesday night, dad came home from work at 7:15 p.m. He walked in sat down and kicked off his shoes. He said, I need a vacation. Let's go to aunt Mimis house at the ~~beeche~~ beach. I want to leave at 1:00 p.m. on friday"

mom said great! Ill call Aunt mimi now.

Error Summary

Capitalization	11
Punctuation:	
Apostrophe	2
Comma	6
Period	1
Quotation Mark	3
Other	2
Spelling	1

MONDAY WEEK 8

friday june 11 2004

dear diary

what a terrible day I got up at 658 a.m. We ate breakfast packed the car and waited. The pet sitters bike had a flat. We didn't leave until 942 a.m.

every ten ~~minnits~~ minutes, pete said are we there yet, dad? We finally arrived at 5;26 p.m.

Error Summary

Capitalization	9
Punctuation:	
Apostrophe	1
Comma	6
Quotation Mark	2
Other	4
Spelling	1

TUESDAY WEEK 8

Name ______________________________

Rosie's Diary

wednesday june 9. 2004

dear diary

On tuesday night, dad came home from work at 7:15 p.m. He walked in sat down and kicked off his shoes. He said, I need a vacation. Let's go to aunt Mimis house at the beeche. I want to leave at 1-00 p.m. on friday"

mom said great Ill call Aunt mimi now.

WATCH FOR

- colons in time
- dialog
- exclamations

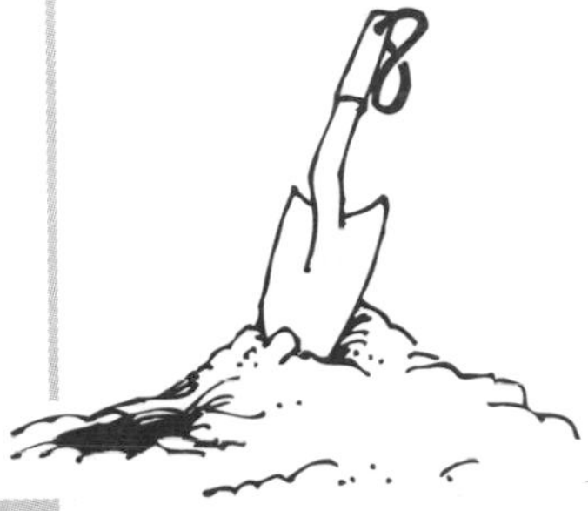

MONDAY **WEEK 8**

friday june 11- 2004

dear diary

what a terrible day I got up at 658 a.m. We ate breakfast packed the car and waited. The pet sitters bike had a flat. We didn't leave until 942 a.m.

every ten minnits, pete said are we there yet, dad? We finally arrived at 5;26 p.m.

WATCH FOR

- colons in time
- dialog
- exclamations

TUESDAY **WEEK 8**

saturday june 12 2004
dear diary;

this morning at 9 14 a.m. I rode my cousin Mikes bike to the beach. It was beautiful. I swam collected shells and read. soon, the rest of the family joined me.

I asked, auntie, can we watch the sunset tonight?

aunt mimi said sure We'll come back at 730.

Error Summary	
Capitalization	10
Punctuation:	
Apostrophe	1
Comma	7
Period	1
Quotation Mark	3
Other	2

WEDNESDAY **WEEK 8**

monday june 14 2004
dear, diary

we went out in my aunts boat. at 11,13 a.m., I saw four dolphins. Wow We took pictures sang and chatted. I told aunt mimi that i didn't want to ~~leev~~ leave.

She said "you can stay here until july 1st.

mom and dad nodded I yelled "hooray!

Error Summary	
Capitalization	14
Punctuation:	
Apostrophe	1
Comma	7
Period	1
Quotation Mark	2
Other	2
Spelling	1

THURSDAY **WEEK 8**

Name ______________________________

saturday june 12 2004

dear diary;

this morning at 9"14 a.m. I rode my cousin Mikes bike to the beach. It was beautiful. I swam collected shells and read. soon, the rest of the family joined me.

I asked, auntie, can we watch the sunset tonight?

aunt mimi said "sure We'll come back at 730.

WATCH FOR

- colons in time
- dialog

WEDNESDAY **WEEK 8**

monday june 14 2004

dear, diary

we went out in my aunts boat. at 11,13 a.m., I saw four dolphins. Wow We took pictures sang and chatted. I told aunt mimi that i didn't want to leev.

She said "you can stay here until july 1st.

mom and dad nodded I yelled "hooray!

WATCH FOR

- colons in time
- dialog

THURSDAY **WEEK 8**

Preview the 4 daily lessons to ensure you review or introduce skills that may be unfamiliar to students.

Recommended Reading

have you ever dreamed about being a hero? Well, the kids in Defenders of the universe, a book by D. V. Kelleher, make that dream come true. Each kid has a secret identity, a costume, and a talent. For example, Packrat carries a lot of things in her ~~backpac~~ backpack. the names are clever, and the costumes are great.

Error Summary

Capitalization	3
Punctuation:	
Comma	6
Period	4
Other	2
Spelling	1

MONDAY WEEK 9

The friends are just playing at first, but then they see a ~~womann~~ woman get hit by a car. The driver doesn't stop. The kids use their talents, and they help the police find the driver. How? Read the book to find out. It has suspense, humor, and mystery. The kids sound like real kids. honestly, you'll like Defenders of the Universe.

Error Summary

Capitalization	1
Punctuation:	
Apostrophe	1
Comma	4
Period	2
Other	1
Spelling	1

TUESDAY WEEK 9

Name ____________________

Recommended Reading

have you ever dreamed about being a hero Well the kids in Defenders of the universe a book by D V Kelleher make that dream come true Each kid has a secret identity a costume and a talent. For example, Packrat carries a lot of things in her backpac. the names are clever and the costumes are great

WATCH FOR

- titles of books
- commas

MONDAY **WEEK 9**

The friends are just playing at first but then they see a womann get hit by a car. The driver doesnt stop The kids use their talents and they help the police find the driver. How? Read the book to find out It has suspense humor and mystery. The kids sound like real kids. honestly, you'll like Defenders of the Universe.

WATCH FOR

- titles of books
- commas

TUESDAY **WEEK 9**

do you like riddles? Do homonyms like "cents," "sense" and "scents" confuse you? If so, the book called Eight ate: A feast of homonym riddles by M terban is for you. The riddles are clever and the pictures are funny funnie. Also, the answers explain the meanings of the homonyms Youll think, laugh and learn when you read this book

Error Summary

Capitalization	6
Punctuation:	
Apostrophe	1
Comma	3
Period	3
Other	1
Spelling	1

WEDNESDAY **WEEK 9**

are you too old for an alphabet book No youre not "the icky bug alphabet book" by J pallotta has interesting facts humor and realistic pictures. Some of the bugs in this book include a ladybug a horsefly and a tarantula. Youll learn a lot and have fun, too. Really, you wont want to Miss this icky book

Error Summary

Capitalization	8
Punctuation:	
Apostrophe	3
Comma	5
Period	3
Other	2

THURSDAY **WEEK 9**

Name ________________________________

do you like riddles? Do homonyms like "cents," "sense" and "scents" confuse you? If so, the book called Eight ate: A feast of homonym riddles by M terban is for you. The riddles are clever and the pictures are funnie. Also, the answers explain the meanings of the homonyms Youll think, laugh and learn when you read this book

WATCH FOR

- titles of books
- commas

WEDNESDAY **WEEK 9**

are you too old for an alphabet book No youre not "the icky bug alphabet book" by J pallotta has interesting facts humor and realistic pictures. Some of the bugs in this book include a ladybug a horsefly and a tarantula. Youll learn a lot and have fun, too. Really, you wont want to Miss this icky book

WATCH FOR

- titles of books
- commas

THURSDAY **WEEK 9**

Preview the 4 daily lessons to ensure you review or introduce skills that may be unfamiliar to students.

Historic United States Capitals

Dover delaware, is the capital of the first state in the United states. The second-oldest state house is there. Dover was named for dover england. Mr eldridge johnson was born in dover. Did you know that he invented one of the first record players! In may, Dover celebrates its history with a big fair called Old dover Days.

Error Summary

Capitalization	9
Punctuation:	
Comma	2
Period	1
Other	1

MONDAY WEEK 10

President abe lincoln was born in kentucky. When he was a young boy, he moved with his family to indiana. He later settled in springfield illinois. Mr lincoln, Mrs Lincoln, and three of their children are buried there. Many tourists come to see Lincoln's home and grave. In february, theres a Lincoln birthday weekend. There is a big parade. Doesnt that sound like fun? The state fair is held in august.

Error Summary

Capitalization	9
Punctuation:	
Apostrophe	2
Comma	1
Period	2
Other	1

TUESDAY WEEK 10

Name ____________________

Historic United States Capitals

Dover delaware, is the capital of the first state in the United states. The second-oldest state house is there. Dover was named for dover england. Mr eldridge johnson was born in dover. Did you know that he invented one of the first record players! In may, Dover celebrates its history with a big fair called Old dover Days.

WATCH FOR

- names of places and people
- questions

MONDAY **WEEK 10**

President abe lincoln was born in kentucky. When he was a young boy, he moved with his family to indiana. He later settled in springfield illinois. Mr lincoln, Mrs Lincoln, and three of their children are buried there. Many tourists come to see Lincoln's home and grave. In february, theres' a Lincoln birthday weekend. There is a big parade. Doesnt that sound like fun The state fair is held in august.

WATCH FOR

- names of places and people
- questions

TUESDAY **WEEK 10**

Would you like to see juneau alaska? Youll have to go by boat, airplane, or dog sled! Juneau doesn't have any roads. Its' the only U.S. capital like that. The City was started in 1888. It was named for Mr. joseph juneau. He and others found over $158 million worth of gold there. Do you like folk festivals juneau has a great one in april

Error Summary

Capitalization	7
Punctuation:	
Apostrophe	2
Comma	1
Period	2
Other	2

WEDNESDAY **WEEK 10**

honolulu hawai`i, is the capital of the newest state. It has the oldest wooden house on the islands. The only palace in the U.S. is there. Two rooms in the capitol building look like volcano cones. Theres a museum for the battleship USS Arizona. It sank in nearby pearl harbor. Wouldn't you like to surf in the pacific Ocean off hawai`i

Error Summary

Capitalization	6
Punctuation:	
Apostrophe	1
Comma	1
Other	2

THURSDAY **WEEK 10**

Name ____

Would you like to see juneau alaska Youll have to go by boat, airplane, or dog sled! Juneau doesn't have any roads. Its' the only U.S. capital like that. The City was started in 1888. It was named for M.r. joseph juneau. He and others found over $158 million worth of gold there. Do you like folk festivals juneau has a great one in april

WATCH FOR
- names of people and places
- questions

WEDNESDAY **WEEK 10**

honolulu hawai`i, is the capital of the newest state. It has the oldest wooden house on the islands. The only palace in the U.S. is there. Two rooms in the capitol building look like volcano cones. Theres a museum for the battleship USS Arizona. It sank in nearby pearl harbor. Wouldn't you like to surf in the pacific Ocean off hawai`i

WATCH FOR
- names of places and ships

THURSDAY **WEEK 10**

Preview the 4 daily lessons to ensure you review or introduce skills that may be unfamiliar to students.

Kids on the Go

Wanda Know ~~rights~~ writes for the magazine kids today. here, she ~~interview~~ interviews Bea Gone of the organization Travel Kids.

WK: Where did you celebrate presidents' day?

BG: That was february 17, 2003. We toured George Washington's home at mount vernon, virginia. We sang "yankee doodle dandy" and ate cherry pie.

Error Summary

Capitalization	12
Language Usage	1
Punctuation:	
Comma	2
Period	1
Quotation Mark	2
Other	2
Spelling	1

MONDAY **WEEK 11**

WK: Where did you go for independence day?

BG: We went to philadelphia, pennsylvania, on july 4, 2003. We watched a parade and sang "the star spangled banner." We saw a movie called 1776. We took a tour of the USS Olympia. It's a historic ship and museum. During the fireworks, we sang "it's a grand old flag."

Error Summary

Capitalization	13
Punctuation:	
Apostrophe	1
Comma	2
Period	1
Quotation Mark	3
Other	3

TUESDAY **WEEK 11**

Name ______________________________

Kids on the Go

Wanda Know rights for the magazine kids today. here, she interview Bea Gone of the organization Travel Kids

WK: Where did you celebrate presidents' day

BG: That was february 17 2003. We toured George Washington's home at mount vernon virginia. We sang yankee doodle dandy and ate cherry pie.

WATCH FOR

- questions
- titles of magazines and songs
- holidays

MONDAY | **WEEK 11**

WK: Where did you go for independence day

BG: We went to philadelphia pennsylvania, on july 4 2003. We watched a parade and sang the star spangled banner. We saw a movie called 1776. We took a tour of the USS Olympia. It's a historic ship and museum. During the fireworks, we sang "its a grand old flag

WATCH FOR

- questions
- titles of movies and songs
- holidays
- names of ships

TUESDAY | **WEEK 11**

WK: Where did you go for Earth Day on april 22 2004

BG: We went to san francisco california. We read "the Earth book" to school kids. We sang every living thing.

WK: Wasn't that written for Earth day's founder

BG: Yes. We heard more ~~abowt~~ about John McConnell while we toured the bay aboard the Golden Gate Cruiser.

Error Summary

Capitalization	10
Punctuation:	
Comma	2
Quotation Mark	2
Other	4
Spelling	1

WEDNESDAY **WEEK 11**

WK: Did you go to lincoln nebraska, for arbor day

BG: Yes. arbor day began in nebraska. We went there on april 25 2004. We planted ~~treas~~ trees in a new park.

WK: Did you read poems like trees and "Evergreen?

BG: Yes, and we saw a movie called all about arbor day.

WK: Thanks for the interview. I'll talk to you again soon?

Error Summary

Capitalization	13
Punctuation:	
Comma	2
Period	1
Quotation Mark	3
Other	3
Spelling	1

THURSDAY **WEEK 11**

Name ______________________________

WK: Where did you go for Earth Day on april 22 2004

BG: We went to san francisco california. We read "the Earth book" to school kids. We sang every living thing.

WK: Wasn't that written for Earth day's founder

BG: Yes. We heard more abowt John McConnell while we toured the bay aboard the Golden Gate Cruiser.

WATCH FOR

- questions
- titles of books and songs
- holidays
- names of ships

WEDNESDAY **WEEK 11**

WK: Did you go to lincoln nebraska, for arbor day

BG: Yes. arbor day began in nebraska. We went there on april 25 2004. We planted treas in a new park.

WK: Did you read poems like trees and "Evergreen.

BG: Yes, and we saw a movie called all about arbor day.

WK: Thanks for the interview. I'll talk to you again soon?

WATCH FOR

- questions
- titles of poems and movies
- holidays

THURSDAY **WEEK 11**

Preview the 4 daily lessons to ensure you review or introduce skills that may be unfamiliar to students.

John Glenn, Space Hero

John glenn was the first American to orbit Earth in a spacecraft. The Friendship 7 was launched from Cape Canaveral, florida, on february 20 ^ 1962. It went around earth three ~~tims~~ times. Then it splashed down in the atlantic Ocean. The United States Navy ship Noa picked john up. He was safe! John glenn became a hero.

Error Summary	
Capitalization	7
Punctuation:	
Comma	1
Other	2
Spelling	1

MONDAY WEEK 12

John was born on july 18 ^ 1921, in cambridge, Ohio. He ~~wint~~ went to college. john then became a Marine Corps pilot. He fought in two wars. he got many medals for his service. on april 9 ^ 1959, John became one of the first astronauts. At first, he was a backup pilot. He provided backup for astronauts virgil Grissom and Alan shephard.

Error Summary	
Capitalization	8
Punctuation:	
Comma	2
Spelling	1

TUESDAY WEEK 12

Name ______________________________

John Glenn, Space Hero

John glenn was the first American to orbit Earth in a spacecraft. The Friendship 7 was launched from Cape Canaveral, florida, on february 20 1962. It went around earth three tims. Then it splashed down in the atlantic Ocean. The United States Navy ship Noa picked john up. He was safe! John glenn became a hero.

WATCH FOR

- names of places, spacecraft, and ships
- dates

MONDAY **WEEK 12**

John was born on july 18 1921, in cambridge, Ohio. He wint to college. john then became a Marine Corps pilot. He fought in two wars. he got many medals for his service. on april 9 1959, John became one of the first astronauts. At first, he was a backup pilot. He provided backup for astronauts virgil Grissom and Alan shephard.

WATCH FOR

- names of places
- dates

TUESDAY **WEEK 12**

John did other work for the space program. He helped design cockpits for the Apollo spacecraft. John retired from the space program on january 16, 1964. He retired from the Marine Corps on january 1, 1965. In 1974, john became a United States senator for the state of ohio. He served in the Senate for twenty twenny-five years.

Error Summary

Capitalization	4
Punctuation:	
Comma	2
Period	1
Spelling	1

WEDNESDAY **WEEK 12**

On october 29, 1998, John became the oldest person to fly in space. He was a crew member on the Discovery, a space shuttle. He wanted to see sea how space affected older people. Vice President al Gore watched the launch at a school named for glenn. The shuttle landed in florida on november 7, 1998. At 77, John was a hero again.

Error Summary

Capitalization	5
Punctuation:	
Comma	3
Other	1
Spelling	1

THURSDAY **WEEK 12**

Name ______________________________

John did other work for the space program He helped design cockpits for the Apollo spacecraft. John retired from the space program on january 16 1964. He retired from the Marine Corps on january 1 1965. In 1974, john became a United States senator for the state of ohio. He served in the Senate for twenny-five years.

WATCH FOR

- names of places
- dates

WEDNESDAY **WEEK 12**

On october 29 1998, John became the oldest person to fly in space. He was a crew member on the Discovery a space shuttle. He wanted to sea how space affected older people. Vice President al Gore watched the launch at a school named for glenn. The shuttle landed in florida on november 7 1998. At 77, John was a hero again.

WATCH FOR

- names of places and spacecraft
- dates

THURSDAY **WEEK 12**

Preview the 4 daily lessons to ensure you review or introduce skills that may be unfamiliar to students.

Chief Seattle and the Settlers

Seattle saw his first white man ~~wen~~ when he was a young boy. A ship called the HMS Discovery sailed into Puget Sound. Seattle lived there with his tribe. Seattle's father, chief schweabe, took him on board the ship. captain George vancouver gave Seattle a treat. seattle decided that some white people were nice.

Error Summary	
Capitalization	5
Punctuation:	
Apostrophe	1
Comma	1
Other	1
Spelling	1

MONDAY **WEEK 13**

At 21, Seattle became the tribe's chief. By that time, many settlers were moving to the Pacific Northwest. They liked the Puget sound area. Seattle invited Isaac N. Ebey and B. F. Shaw to live there. He ~~tawt~~ taught the settler's to fish for salmon, and he helped them build houses. In the winter, he gave them food.

Error Summary	
Capitalization	1
Punctuation:	
Apostrophe	1
Comma	1
Period	1
Spelling	2

TUESDAY **WEEK 13**

Name ______________________________

Chief Seattle and the Settlers

Seattle saw his first white man wen he was a young boy. A ship called the HMS Discovery sailed into Puget Sound. Seattle lived there with his tribe. Seattles father, chief schweabe took him on board the ship. captain George vancouver gave Seattle a treat. seattle decided that some white people were nice.

WATCH FOR

- names of ships and people
- commas

MONDAY **WEEK 13**

At 21, Seattle became the tribes chief. By that time, many settlers were moving to the Pacific Northwest. They liked the Puget sound area. Seattle invited Isaac N. Ebey and B. F Shaw to live there. He tawt the settler's to fish for salmon and he helped them build houses. In the winter, he gave them food.

WATCH FOR

- people's names and initials
- commas

TUESDAY **WEEK 13**

chief Seattle started a fishery with Mr. charles Fay. He was from San francisco. Seattle and mr. David S maynard then opened a fishery. It was near the shore of Elliott bay. Many settlers moved there. They liked the ~~helpfull~~ helpful chief, so they named their town after him. seattle is now the biggest city in washington state.

Error Summary

Capitalization	9
Punctuation:	
Comma	1
Period	1
Spelling	1

WEDNESDAY **WEEK 13**

Soon, the United States' wanted to ~~bye~~ buy his tribe's land. Chief Seattle met with Territorial Governor isaac stevens at Point elliott. They signed a treaty, and Seattle sold over two million acres of land. The land became the white settlers' land. Until his ~~deth~~ death, chief Seattle kept his friendship with the settlers.

Error Summary

Capitalization	4
Punctuation:	
Apostrophe	2
Comma	1
Spelling	2

THURSDAY **WEEK 13**

Name ________________________________

chief Seattle started a fishery with Mr. charles Fay. He was from San francisco. Seattle and mr. David S maynard then opened a fishery. It was near the shore of Elliott bay. Many settlers moved there. They liked the helpfull chief so they named their town after him. seattle is now the biggest city in washington state.

WATCH FOR

- people's names, initials, and titles
- commas

WEDNESDAY **WEEK 13**

Soon, the United States' wanted to bye his tribe's land. Chief Seattle met with Territorial Governor isaac stevens at Point elliott. They signed a treaty and Seattle sold over two million acres of land. The land became the white settlers land. Until his deth, chief Seattle kept his friendship with the settlers.

WATCH FOR

- people's names and titles
- commas

THURSDAY **WEEK 13**

Preview the 4 daily lessons to ensure you review or introduce skills that may be unfamiliar to students.

Shea and the Leprechaun

"happy St. Patrick's Day, mom! i am going to ~~ketch~~ catch a leprechaun!" shouted Shea.

"good luck, its tricky!" said her mother. Shea got her dog, Jigs. They ran to the field of wild damp grass.

"once granny said she almost caught a leprechaun here," Shea told Jigs. "Lets find him. i want his gold."

Error Summary

Capitalization	8
Punctuation:	
Apostrophe	2
Comma	1
Period	1
Spelling	1

MONDAY WEEK 14

Suddenly, Shea heard a low quiet laugh coming from behind a tall broad tree. "that may be the leprechaun granny saw," she said to Jigs. "Dont bark while i look."

Shea peeked around the tree she saw a tiny knee-high man in green clothes she ran from behind the tree and ~~grabed~~ grabbed him. Shea said, "leprechaun! i want your gold!"

Error Summary

Capitalization	7
Punctuation:	
Apostrophe	1
Comma	3
Period	2
Spelling	1

TUESDAY WEEK 14

Name ______________________________

Shea and the Leprechaun

"happy St. Patrick's Day, mom! i am going to ketch a leprechaun!" shouted Shea.

"good luck, its tricky!" said her mother. Shea got her dog, Jigs. They ran to the field of wild damp grass.

"once granny said she almost caught a leprechaun here," Shea told Jigs. "Lets find him. i want his gold."

WATCH FOR

- dialog
- commas

MONDAY **WEEK 14**

Suddenly, Shea heard a low quiet laugh coming from behind a tall broad tree. "that may be the leprechaun granny saw," she said to Jigs. "Dont bark while i look."

Shea peeked around the tree she saw a tiny knee-high man in green clothes she ran from behind the tree and grabed him. Shea said, "leprechaun! i want your gold!"

WATCH FOR

- dialog
- commas

TUESDAY **WEEK 14**

"you caught me! Youre much quicker than granny," said the leprechaun. "let go of me and I will tell you where to find a full heavy bag of gold."

Shea let ~~lett~~ go. "go to the smooth round rock in the center of the buttercup patch. Thats where ~~whare~~ the gold is," he told her. "now its all yours. Youll be very, very rich."

Error Summary

Capitalization	5
Punctuation:	
Apostrophe	4
Comma	2
Spelling	2

WEDNESDAY **WEEK 14**

Shea and Jigs searched ~~serched~~ all around. They didnt find gold. All they saw was a field of silky fluttering flowers. Shea ran back ~~backe~~ to the tree, but the leprechaun wasnt there.

"next time, I wont be fooled!" she yelled into the air. "now its time to go home," she said to Jigs. "Well tell mom, dad, and granny. Theyll have ideas for next year."

Error Summary

Capitalization	5
Punctuation:	
Apostrophe	6
Comma	1
Spelling	2

THURSDAY **WEEK 14**

Name ______________________________

"you caught me! Youre much quicker than granny," said the leprechaun. "let go of me and I will tell you where to find a full heavy bag of gold."

Shea lett go. "go to the smooth round rock in the center of the buttercup patch. Thats whare the gold is," he told her. "now its all yours. Youll be very, very rich."

WATCH FOR

- dialog
- commas

WEDNESDAY **WEEK 14**

Shea and Jigs serched all around. They didnt find gold. All they saw was a field of silky fluttering flowers. Shea ran backe to the tree, but the leprechaun wasnt there.

"next time, I wont be fooled!" she yelled into the air. "now its time to go home," she said to Jigs. "Well tell mom, dad, and granny. Theyll have ideas for next year."

WATCH FOR

- dialog
- commas

THURSDAY **WEEK 14**

Preview the 4 daily lessons to ensure you review or introduce skills that may be unfamiliar to students.

Undercover Bugs

A patch of ~~berrys~~ berries gleams in the sun. you would ~~loves~~ love to taste a ripe berry. You stop to look for the best one. Then a branch on the bush ~~seeming~~ seems to move. surprise! The branch is not really moving. it is an insect! You have just met a walking stick. Can you guess why it ~~have~~ has that name?

Error Summary	
Capitalization	3
Language Usage	3
Punctuation:	
Period	1
Other	1
Spelling	1

MONDAY WEEK 15

walking sticks are insects that look like twigs or ~~tiney~~ tiny branches. They ~~has~~ have six legs. some walking sticks can fold up their legs to look even more like a twig. Did you know that they eat only leaves? Some like berry leaves. others ~~eats~~ eat cherry leaves. Some people keep walking sticks as pets. some of these pets eat lettuce leaves.

Error Summary	
Capitalization	4
Language Usage	2
Punctuation:	
Period	2
Other	1
Spelling	1

TUESDAY WEEK 15

Name ____

Undercover Bugs

A patch of berrys gleams in the sun. you would loves to taste a ripe berry. You stop to look for the best one. Then a branch on the bush seeming to move. surprise! The branch is not really moving it is an insect! You have just met a walking stick. Can you guess why it have that name

![WATCH FOR]

- questions

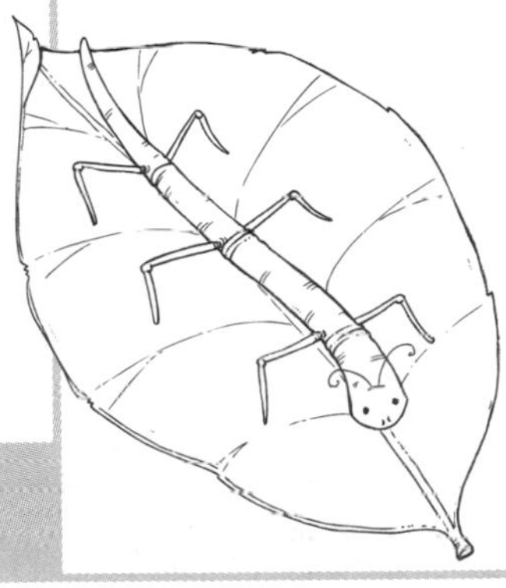

MONDAY WEEK 15

walking sticks are insects that look like twigs or tiney branches. They has six legs. some walking sticks can fold up their legs to look even more like a twig. Did you know that they eat only leaves. Some like berry leaves others eats cherry leaves. Some people keep walking sticks as pets some of these pets eat lettuce leaves.

WATCH FOR

- questions

TUESDAY WEEK 15

The longest insect in the world ~~are~~ is a walking stick. it's about 13 ~~inchus~~ inches long. Walking sticks that are kept as pets are not usually that big Pet walking sticks may grow to be about 6 inches long. When they first ~~comes~~ come out of their hard eggshells, they can be as small as half an inch. have you ever ~~saw~~ seen anything that small?

Error Summary	
Capitalization	2
Language Usage	3
Punctuation:	
Period	1
Other	1
Spelling	1

WEDNESDAY **WEEK 15**

As insects grow, they ~~sheds~~ shed their hard outer covering. as the walking stick becomes too small for its growing body, a new, bigger covering ~~taking~~ takes the place of the old one. a walking stick may shed its covering up to five times before it becomes an adult. Some ~~teechers~~ teachers keep walking sticks as class pets do you think you would like one in your class?

Error Summary	
Capitalization	3
Language Usage	2
Punctuation:	
Period	1
Other	1
Spelling	1

THURSDAY **WEEK 15**

Name ____________________

The longest insect in the world are a walking stick. it's about 13 inchus long. Walking sticks that are kept as pets are not usually that big Pet walking sticks may grow to be about 6 inches long. When they first comes out of their hard eggshells, they can be as small as half an inch. have you ever saw anything that small

WATCH FOR

• questions

WEDNESDAY **WEEK 15**

As insects grow, they sheds their hard outer covering. as the walking stick becomes too small for its growing body, a new, bigger covering taking the place of the old one. a walking stick may shed its covering up to five times before it becomes an adult. Some teechers keep walking sticks as class pets do you think you would like one in your class

WATCH FOR

• questions

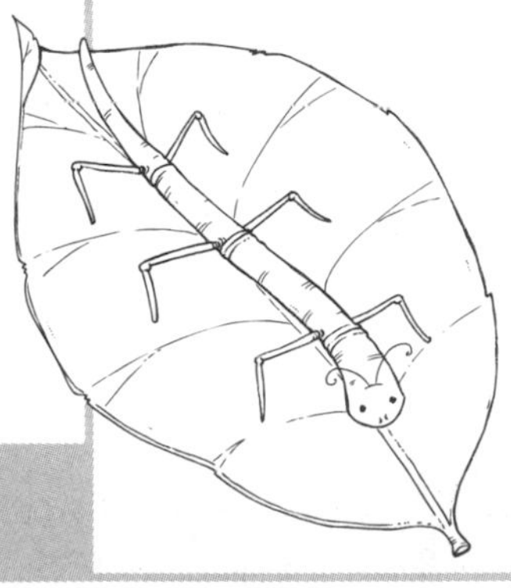

THURSDAY **WEEK 15**

Preview the 4 daily lessons to ensure you review or introduce skills that may be unfamiliar to students.

Short Tall Tales

"Babes Disappearing River" by mr. S P royce

One hot dry June, babe and paul were in oregon. Babe had gone for six and two-thirds days without water. He saw a clean sparkling river. Babe drank for one and one half hour's. He drank nine tenths of the water. That river is now ~~ownly~~ only two and three fourths feet deep.

Error Summary

Capitalization	5
Punctuation:	
Apostrophe	1
Comma	2
Period	2
Other	3
Spelling	2

MONDAY WEEK 16

"babe goes dancing by Ms R M brown"

Babe was in minnesota in july. paul bunyan was playing the fiddle. babe liked Pauls cheerful lively ~~musick~~ music. He danced for five and one half days. His dancing heavy feet made 10,000 holes in the ground. Then it rained for four fifths of a month. The holes became lake's.

Error Summary

Capitalization	9
Punctuation:	
Apostrophe	1
Comma	2
Period	3
Quotation Mark	2
Other	2
Spelling	2

TUESDAY WEEK 16

Name ____________________

Short Tall Tales

"Babes Disappearing River" by mr. S P royce

One hot dry June, babe and paul were in oregon. Babe had gone for six and two-thirds days without water. He saw a clean sparkling river. Babe drank for one and one half hour's. He drank nine tenths of the water. That river is now ownly two and three fourths feet deep.

WATCH FOR
- story titles
- commas
- hyphens

MONDAY WEEK 16

"babe goes dancing by Ms R M brown"

Babe was in minnesota in july. paul bunyan was playing the fiddle. babe liked Pauls cheerful lively musick. He danced for five and one half days. His dancing heavy feet made 10,000 holes in the ground. Then it rained for four fifths of a month. The holes became lake's.

WATCH FOR
- story titles
- commas
- hyphens

TUESDAY WEEK 16

"paul and babe in Hollywood by ms. J A mills

Paul and babe went to hollywood in may. They were on amazing people and pets the TV show. There was a strong scary earthquake. Five sixths of california fell into the pacific ocean. Paul and babe put it back. They then starred in a movie called california's heroes.

Error Summary	
Capitalization	16
Punctuation:	
Comma	2
Period	2
Quotation Mark	1
Other	3

WEDNESDAY **WEEK 16**

Babe helps johnny inkslinger" by Mr J D post

Johnnys fountain pen broke in march. babe went to the Everglades in florida. He brought back some stalks of dry hollow grass. Each one was about three fifths of a mile long. johnny filled one with nine hundred and two thirds gallons of ink. He wrote and sang "Babes ballad.

Error Summary	
Capitalization	9
Punctuation:	
Apostrophe	2
Comma	1
Period	3
Quotation Mark	2
Other	2

THURSDAY **WEEK 16**

Name ______________________________

"paul and babe in Hollywood by ms. J A mills

Paul and babe went to hollywood in may. They were on amazing people and pets the TV show. There was a strong scary earthquake. Five sixths of california fell into the pacific ocean. Paul and babe put it back. They then starred in a movie called california's heroes.

WATCH FOR

- story titles
- titles of TV shows
- commas
- hyphens

WEDNESDAY **WEEK 16**

Babe helps johnny inkslinger" by Mr J D post

Johnnys fountain pen broke in march. babe went to the Everglades in florida. He brought back some stalks of dry hollow grass. Each one was about three fifths of a mile long. johnny filled one with nine hundred and two thirds gallons of ink. He wrote and sang "Babes ballad.

WATCH FOR

- story and song titles
- commas
- hyphens

THURSDAY **WEEK 16**

Preview the 4 daily lessons to ensure you review or introduce skills that may be unfamiliar to students.

Hand-Me-Downs

On monday, an enormous carton arrived for ginny. It was from peggy and tina her cousins. The ~~karten~~ carton was full of their used clothes.

ginny said mom do i have to keep these clothes? I don't like Peggys old sweaters. I don't want to wear Tinas jeans.

Error Summary

Capitalization	7
Punctuation:	
Apostrophe	2
Comma	3
Quotation Mark	2
Other	1
Spelling	1

MONDAY **WEEK 17**

mom said "ginny won't you please wear them!? Your cousins clothes are like new, and they're the ~~write~~ right size.

ginny said, "okay mom. I would just like to have something new, too.

"mom said, would you like to go shopping on saturday? We can find something to go with the clothes."

Error Summary

Capitalization	8
Punctuation:	
Apostrophe	1
Comma	3
Quotation Mark	4
Other	2
Spelling	1

TUESDAY **WEEK 17**

Name ____________________________________

Hand-Me-Downs

On monday, an enormous carton arrived for ginny. It was from peggy and tina her cousins. The karten was full of their used clothes.

ginny said mom do i have to keep these clothes. I don't like Peggys old sweaters. I don't want to wear Tinas jeans.

WATCH FOR

- commas
- dialog
- questions

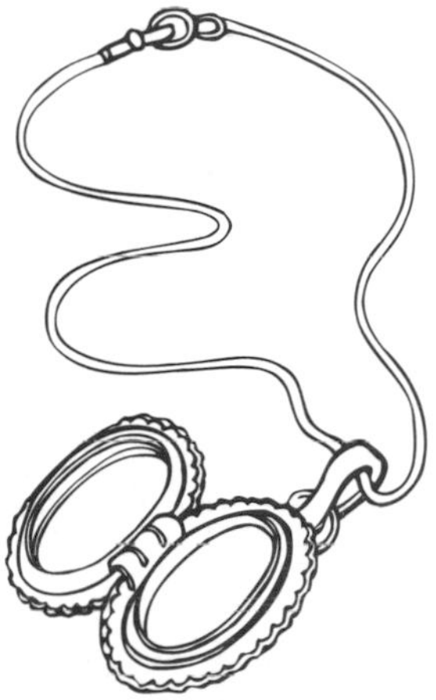

MONDAY **WEEK 17**

mom said "ginny won't you please wear them! Your cousins clothes are like new, and they're the write size.

ginny said, "okay mom. I would just like to have something new, too.

"mom said, would you like to go shopping on saturday. We can find something to go with the clothes."

WATCH FOR

- commas
- dialog
- questions

TUESDAY **WEEK 17**

ginny "said," can we really? Thanks, mom."

On saturday, they went shopping. ginny held up a ~~pear~~ pair of suspenders and a T-shirt. She said, "mom, I think these would look super with Tina's jeans."

mom said, "marvelous! How do you like this skirt? It matches one of Peggy's sweaters. Let's buy everything."

Error Summary

Capitalization	8
Punctuation:	
Apostrophe	2
Comma	4
Quotation Mark	7
Other	2
Spelling	1

WEDNESDAY **WEEK 17**

On sunday, mom said, "ginny, this is another hand-me-down." She showed ginny a silver locket. mom said, "this was Nana's and then Grandmother's. grandmother gave it to me. It will be yours someday."

ginny said, "thanks, Mom. Your family's locket is special. Now I understand a hand-me-down's importance."

Error Summary

Capitalization	9
Punctuation:	
Apostrophe	4
Comma	4
Quotation Mark	5

THURSDAY **WEEK 17**

Name ______________________________

ginny “said,” can we really. Thanks mom.

On saturday, they went shopping. ginny held up a pear of suspenders and a T-shirt. She said “mom I think these would look super with Tinas jeans.

mom said marvelous! How do you like this skirt. It matches one of Peggys’ sweaters. Let’s buy everything.

WATCH FOR

- commas
- dialog
- questions

WEDNESDAY **WEEK 17**

On sunday, mom said “ginny this is another hand-me-down. She showed ginny a silver locket. mom said, this was Nanas and then Grandmothers. grandmother gave it to me. It will be yours someday.

ginny said thanks Mom. Your familys locket is special. Now I understand a hand-me-dow’ns importance.

WATCH FOR

- commas
- dialog

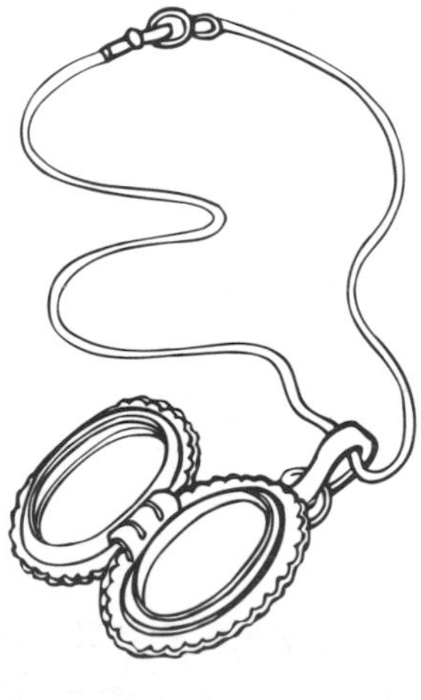

THURSDAY **WEEK 17**

Preview the 4 daily lessons to ensure you review or introduce skills that may be unfamiliar to students.

How to Skate Safely

how do you buy skates? First, wear your skating socks when you try on skates. Second, kick your feet into the backs of the boots. After that, buckle the boots and stand up! Next, make sure your toes aren't squashed. last, make sure your heel doesn't slide up and down.

From Safe skating magazine by Mike Hulon.

Error Summary

Capitalization	4
Punctuation:	
Apostrophe	2
Period	2
Other	1

MONDAY WEEK 18

What kind of safety equipment should you buy? buy wrist guards with plastic plates for wrist protection. Get elbow and knee guards in case of falls. The most important thing is a padded helmet! make sure it's snug. you don't want a head injury. Now you're ~~reddy~~ ready to roll!

From skate equipment today by Tracy Hill

Error Summary

Capitalization	6
Punctuation:	
Apostrophe	3
Period	1
Other	3
Spelling	1

TUESDAY WEEK 18

Name ______________________________

How to Skate Safely

how do you buy skates First, wear your skating socks when you try on skates. Second, kick your feet into the backs of the boots After that, buckle the boots and stand up! Next, make sure your toes arent squashed. last, make sure your heel doesnt slide up and down.

From Safe skating magazine by Mike Hulon

WATCH FOR

- questions
- apostrophes
- magazine titles

MONDAY **WEEK 18**

What kind of safety equipment should you buy buy wrist guards with plastic plates for wrist protection Get elbow and knee guards in case of falls. The most important thing is a padded helmet! make sure its snug. you dont want a head injury. Now youre reddy to roll

From skate equipment today by Tracy Hill

WATCH FOR

- questions
- apostrophes
- magazine titles

TUESDAY **WEEK 18**

how can you skate for fitness? For your safety, go to a flat, paved area! Don't go near traffic. Don't go down hills if you can't stop. do five minutes of slow skating skateing as a warm-up. Next, skate rapidly for twenty minutes. skate slowly for five minutes minnets to cool down. You'll feel super?!

From fitness skating magazine By Kim scott

Error Summary	
Capitalization	8
Punctuation:	
Apostrophe	4
Period	2
Other	3
Spelling	2

WEDNESDAY WEEK 18

How do you fall harmlessly? first, bend forward at the waist. Second, bend your knees. Third, touch your knee guards. Next, slide forward onto your protective gear. keep your head hedd up to avoid facial scrapes. at the same time, let your body slide flat on the ground. You're safe!

From athletic safeguards by Matt todd

Error Summary	
Capitalization	6
Punctuation:	
Apostrophe	1
Period	1
Other	3
Spelling	1

THURSDAY WEEK 18

Name ______________________________

how can you skate for fitness. For your safety, go to a flat, paved area! Don't' go near traffic. Dont go down hills if you cant' stop. do five minutes of slow skateing as a warm-up Next, skate rapidly for twenty minutes. skate slowly for five minnets to cool down. Youll' feel super?

From fitness skating magazine By Kim scott

WATCH FOR

- questions
- apostrophes
- magazine titles

WEDNESDAY **WEEK 18**

How do you fall harmlessly first, bend forward at the waist. Second, bend your knees. Third, touch your knee guards Next, slide forward onto your protective gear. keep your hedd up to avoid facial scrapes. at the same time, let your body slide flat on the ground. Youre safe

From athletic safeguards by Matt todd

WATCH FOR

- questions
- apostrophes
- magazine titles

THURSDAY **WEEK 18**

Preview the 4 daily lessons to ensure you review or introduce skills that may be unfamiliar to students.

Meg's Prize

At 400 p.m one day in 1955, Meg Burns walked into the house and yelled "mom you wont believe this I won a television set! We have the ~~furst~~ first TV on the block!

Doris Burns said my how lucky good for you Meg.

Meg said now we can watch the mighty mouse playhouse and I Love Lucy right here at home.

Error Summary	
Capitalization	7
Punctuation:	
Apostrophe	1
Comma	6
Period	3
Quotation Mark	5
Other	4
Spelling	1

MONDAY WEEK 19

Meg called out dad come look at this Rich come here!

It was 4,30 P.M. and american bandstand was just starting. They heard voices singing "bandstand boogie. Dick Clark appeared on the tiny screen and said hello heres our show for today. Meet our teenage dancers.

Meg said Im going to dance along with them.

Error Summary	
Capitalization	9
Punctuation:	
Apostrophe	2
Comma	5
Period	1
Quotation Mark	7
Other	3

TUESDAY WEEK 19

Name ______________________________

Meg's Prize

At 400 p:m one day in 1955, Meg Burns walked into the house and yelled "mom you wont believe this I won a television set! We have the furst TV on the block!

Doris Burns said my how lucky good for you Meg.

Meg said now we can watch the mighty mouse playhouse and I Love Lucy right here at home.

WATCH FOR

- dialog
- colons in time
- titles of TV shows

MONDAY **WEEK 19**

Meg called out dad come look at this Rich come here!

It was 4,30 P.M. and american bandstand was just starting. They heard voices singing "bandstand boogie. Dick Clark appeared on the tiny screen and said hello heres our show for today. Meet our teenage dancers.

Meg said Im going to dance along with them.

WATCH FOR

- dialog
- colons in time
- titles of TV shows

TUESDAY **WEEK 19**

At 530, Rich wanted to watch The howdy doody show. They all sang along to Its howdy doody time.

Rich said wow! Howdy Doody is a funny puppet. They watched city newsreel from 6,00 until 700 pM. "the milton berle show" was on next. They laughed at the funny actors until 800 P.m

Error Summary

Capitalization	15
Punctuation:	
Apostrophe	1
Comma	1
Period	3
Quotation Mark	6
Other	8

WEDNESDAY **WEEK 19**

The family watched Roy Rogers and Dale Evans ride their horses during The roy rogers Show. At the end of the show, they sang happy trails to you.

At 900 pm, Meg said mom we havent had dinner yet."

we'll have to learn to use this TV wisely said Mrs. Burns. otherwise, well never get anything done!

Error Summary

Capitalization	8
Punctuation:	
Apostrophe	2
Comma	3
Period	2
Quotation Mark	7
Other	3

THURSDAY **WEEK 19**

Name ______________________________

At 530, Rich wanted to watch The howdy doody show. They all sang along to Its howdy doody time.

Rich said wow Howdy Doody is a funny puppet. They watched city newsreel from 6,00 until 700 pM: "the milton berle show" was on next. They laughed at the funny actors until 800 P.m

WATCH FOR

- dialog
- colons in time
- titles of TV shows

WEDNESDAY **WEEK 19**

The family watched Roy Rogers and Dale Evans ride their horses during The roy rogers Show. At the end of the show, they sang happy trails to you.

At 900 pm, Meg said mom we havent had dinner yet."

we'll have to learn to use this TV wisely said Mrs. Burns. otherwise, well never get anything done

WATCH FOR

- dialog
- colons in time
- titles of TV shows

THURSDAY **WEEK 19**

Preview the 4 daily lessons to ensure you review or introduce skills that may be unfamiliar to students.

The Blizzard of 2003

Washington, D.C. February 16, 2003

Residents of the nations capital woke up to a winter wonderland this ~~morening~~ morning. A huge storm system came through West virginia into the washington DC area on saturday. By sunday afternoon, about 60 centimeters (2 ft) of snow ~~cuvvered~~ covered the ground. Cars were stuck on new york Avenue and other streets.

Error Summary	
Capitalization	6
Punctuation:	
Apostrophe	1
Comma	2
Period	3
Spelling	2

MONDAY WEEK 20

bob T Stone was in mt vernon square. He was ~~makeing~~ making a snowman and singing frosty the snowman He said, its great my snowman is 182 centimeters (6 ft) high!

ms meg f moore and her dog were walking on K St to a friends house. Her dog was catching snowflakes and she was ~~singging~~ singing let it snow

Error Summary	
Capitalization	15
Punctuation:	
Apostrophe	2
Comma	1
Period	7
Quotation Mark	6
Other	1
Spelling	2

TUESDAY WEEK 20

Name ______________________________

The Blizzard of 2003

Washington, D.C. February 16, 2003

Residents of the nations capital woke up to a winter wonderland this morening. A huge storm system came through West virginia into the washington DC area on saturday. By sunday afternoon, about 60 centimeters (2 ft) of snow cuvvered the ground. Cars were stuck on new york Avenue and other streets.

WATCH FOR
- names of places
- abbreviations

MONDAY **WEEK 20**

bob T Stone was in mt vernon square. He was makeing a snowman and singing frosty the snowman. He said, its great my snowman is 182 centimeters (6 ft) high

ms meg f moore and her dog were walking on K St to a friends house. Her dog was catching snowflakes and she was singging let it snow.

WATCH FOR
- dialog
- names of places
- abbreviations

TUESDAY **WEEK 20**

jeff g hanks said my cars roof has 71 centimeters (28 in) of snow on it. Iv e never seen scene anything like this! Im from monterey california mr hanks was to fly home today but baltimore-washington international airport is closed. He may not get out until tuesday.

Error Summary

Capitalization	13
Punctuation:	
Apostrophe	3
Comma	3
Period	3
Quotation Mark	2
Other	1
Spelling	1

WEDNESDAY **WEEK 20**

dr ann T green said Four-wheel-drive cars are needed. If drivers can help we're looking for people to give hospital workers rides. We need needs the public's help.

Weather forecaster dave R coons said The storm is moving north and dover delaware, may get 60 centimeters (2 ft,) of snow by monday. Stay inside and keep saif safe."

Error Summary

Capitalization	8
Language Usage	1
Punctuation:	
Comma	5
Period	4
Quotation Mark	3
Spelling	1

THURSDAY **WEEK 20**

Name ______________________________

jeff a hanks said my cars' roof has 71 centimeters (28 in) of snow on it. Iv'e never scene anything like this Im from monterey california. mr hanks was to fly home today but baltimore-washington international airport is closed. He may not get out until tuesday.

WATCH FOR

- dialog
- names of places
- abbreviations

WEDNESDAY **WEEK 20**

dr ann T green said Four-wheel-drive cars are needed. If drivers can help we're looking for people to give hospital workers rides. We needs the public's help.

Weather forecaster dave R coons said The storm is moving north and dover delaware, may get 60 centimeters (2 ft,) of snow by monday. Stay inside and keep saif."

WATCH FOR

- dialog
- names of places
- abbreviations

THURSDAY **WEEK 20**

Preview the 4 daily lessons to ensure you review or introduce skills that may be unfamiliar to students.

How to Make a Sand Sundae

What's a sand sundae? It's a cool way to display a photo. Here's how to make one. First, get the supplies. You'll need several clear plastic glasses, or you can use glass jars. They should be from 10-15 centimeters (4-6 in.) tall. Also, get about 155 grams (5 oz.) of colored sand and 124 grams (4 oz.) of white ~~candil~~ candle wax for each sundae.

Error Summary

Punctuation:

Apostrophe	4
Comma	1
Period	3
Spelling	1

MONDAY WEEK 21

Second, get some 4 by 6 centimeter ($1\frac{1}{2}$ in. by $2\frac{1}{2}$ in.) photos. Place a ~~foto~~ photo against the inside of the glass, but make sure it faces the outside of the glass. Use a little bit of clear tape on the sides of the photo, and it'll stay in place. Use more than one photo if they'll fit.

Error Summary

Punctuation:

Apostrophe	2
Comma	2
Period	2
Spelling	1

TUESDAY WEEK 21

Name ____________________________________

How to Make a Sand Sundae

Whats a sand sundae? Its a cool way to display a photo. Heres how to make one. First, get the supplies. Youll need several clear plastic glasses or you can use glass jars. They should be from 10-15 centimeters (4-6 in) tall. Also, get about 155 grams (5 oz) of colored sand and 124 grams (4 oz) of white candil wax for each sundae.

WATCH FOR
- abbreviations
- commas

MONDAY **WEEK 21**

Second, get some 4 by 6 centimeter ($1\frac{1}{2}$ in by $2\frac{1}{2}$ in) photos. Place a foto against the inside of the glass but make sure it faces the outside of the glass. Use a little bit of clear tape on the sides of the photo and itll stay in place. Use more than one photo if theyll fit.

WATCH FOR
- abbreviations
- commas

TUESDAY **WEEK 21**

Third, add the sand use different colors to make a design. Use about 31 grams (1 oz) each of 4 or 5 colors. To start, put ~~won~~ one color into the glass. Next, add a layer of another color. After that, put in the next color ~~Finaly~~ Finally, add the last color. Tilt the glass to make curves or use a toothpick. To push one color into another.

Error Summary

Capitalization	2
Punctuation:	
Comma	1
Period	3
Spelling	2

WEDNESDAY **WEEK 21**

~~Forth~~ Fourth, make the topping but get help from an adult. To start, melt the candle wax in a pot. Next, ~~beet~~ beat it with ~~a~~ an eggbeater until its foamy. After that, spoon the wax onto the top of the sand. Let it drip over a bit and itll look like real whipped cream. Finally, give your "sand sundae" to someone you like or keep it for yourself!

Error Summary

Language Usage	1
Punctuation:	
Apostrophe	2
Comma	3
Spelling	2

THURSDAY **WEEK 21**

Name ______________________________

Third, add the sand use different colors to make a design. Use about 31 grams (1 oz) each of 4 or 5 colors. To start, put won color into the glass. Next, add a layer of another color. After that, put in the next color Finaly, add the last color. Tilt the glass to make curves or use a toothpick. To push one color into another.

WATCH FOR

- abbreviations
- commas

WEDNESDAY **WEEK 21**

Forth, make the topping but get help from an adult. To start, melt the candle wax in a pot. Next, beet it with a eggbeater until its foamy. After that, spoon the wax onto the top of the sand. Let it drip over a bit and itll look like real whipped cream. Finally, give your "sand sundae" to someone you like or keep it for yourself!

WATCH FOR

- commas

THURSDAY **WEEK 21**

Preview the 4 daily lessons to ensure you review or introduce skills that may be unfamiliar to students.

Poetry Book Reviews

where the sidewalk ends by S. Silverstein has 127 poems about food people animals and other things. mr Silverstein's rhymes are clever and his drawings are funny. "the Crocodiles toothache" has a surprise ending. The unicorn was made into a song. Heres a book to share with your family friends and teachers

Error Summary

Capitalization	7
Punctuation:	
Apostrophe	2
Comma	6
Period	2
Quotation Mark	2
Other	1

MONDAY WEEK 22

grandmother's nursery rhymes by N P Jaramillo has rhymes riddles and lullabies. You can ~~reed~~ read them in English or you can read them in Spanish "Grandfathers Poem" is gentle. the spider" is a riddle about nature. You'll enjoy reading ms Jaramillos rhymes and youll be delighted by ms Savadier's colorful drawings.

Error Summary

Capitalization	7
Punctuation:	
Apostrophe	3
Comma	4
Period	5
Quotation Mark	1
Other	1
Spelling	1

TUESDAY WEEK 22

Name ____________________

Poetry Book Reviews

where the sidewalk ends by S. Silverstein has 127 poems about food people animals and other things. mr Silverstein's rhymes are clever and his drawings are funny. "the Crocodiles toothache" has a surprise ending. The unicorn was made into a song. Heres a book to share with your family friends and teachers

WATCH FOR

- titles of books and poems
- commas

MONDAY **WEEK 22**

grandmother's nursery rhymes by N P Jaramillo has rhymes riddles and lullabies. You can reed them in English or you can read them in Spanish "Grandfathers Poem" is gentle. the spider" is a riddle about nature. You'll enjoy reading ms Jaramillos rhymes and youll be delighted by ms Savadier's colorful drawings.

WATCH FOR

- titles of books and poems
- commas

TUESDAY **WEEK 22**

The funny poems in A Poem for a Pickle by E Merriam will make you giggle laugh and chuckle. The poems have a great beat and youll want to dance while you read them. The poem "urban rainbow describes colors in the city. The book Can a can has words with more than one meaning Youd better read this great book

Error Summary

Capitalization	3
Punctuation:	
Apostrophe	2
Comma	3
Period	3
Quotation Mark	1
Other	2

WEDNESDAY　　WEEK 22

The book The dragons are singing tonight by J prelutsky has 17 poems for dragon fans. mr Prelutsky's poems rhyme and they are fun to say aloud. Theres an upset dragon in the poem "A Dragons lament The dragon in Im an amiable dragon" is friendly. You should get this book and then you should read it to your ~~favrit~~ favorite dragon

Error Summary

Capitalization	9
Punctuation:	
Apostrophe	3
Comma	2
Period	3
Quotation Mark	2
Other	1
Spelling	1

THURSDAY　　WEEK 22

Name ______________________________

The funny poems in A Poem for a Pickle by E Merriam will make you giggle laugh and chuckle. The poems have a great beat and youll want to dance while you read them. The poem "urban rainbow describes colors in the city. The book Can a can has words with more than one meaning Youd' better read this great book

WATCH FOR

- titles of books and poems
- commas

WEDNESDAY **WEEK 22**

The book The dragons are singing tonight by J prelutsky has 17 poems for dragon fans. mr Prelutsky's poems rhyme and they are fun to say aloud. Theres an upset dragon in the poem "A Dragons lament. The dragon in Im an amiable dragon" is friendly. You should get this book and then you should read it to your favrit dragon

WATCH FOR

- titles of books and poems
- commas

THURSDAY **WEEK 22**

Preview the 4 daily lessons to ensure you review or introduce skills that may be unfamiliar to students.

The Boston Tea Party

in 1773, the king of england put a tax on the paper paint lead glass and tea sent to the colonies in america.

"we cant vote for or against the tax, so we should'nt have to pay it the colonists in boston said to each other. they refused to buy the taxed goods after a while, the British took away all but the tax on tea.

Error Summary

Capitalization	7
Punctuation:	
Apostrophe	2
Comma	5
Period	1
Quotation Mark	1

MONDAY WEEK 23

the colonists wouldnt buy the tea or pay the tax One evening, angry people gathered in the meeting house. A man yelled "the hated tea is now on ships in our harbor!

someone shouted lets show King George how we feel!"

"boston harbor will be a teapot tonight! cried the crowd.

Error Summary

Capitalization	6
Punctuation:	
Apostrophe	2
Comma	2
Period	1
Quotation Mark	3
Other	3

TUESDAY WEEK 23

Name ____________________

The Boston Tea Party

in 1773, the king of england put a tax on the paper paint lead glass and tea sent to the colonies in america.

"we cant vote for or against the tax, so we should'nt have to pay it the colonists in boston said to each other. they refused to buy the taxed goods after a while, the British took away all but the tax on tea.

WATCH FOR

- dialog
- commas

MONDAY **WEEK 23**

the colonists wouldnt buy the tea or pay the tax One evening, angry people gathered in the meeting house. A man yelled "the hated tea is now on ships in our harbor

someone shouted lets show King George how we feel."

"boston harbor will be a teapot tonight cried the crowd.

WATCH FOR

- dialog
- exclamations

TUESDAY **WEEK 23**

A ~~groope~~ group of men dressed up like Indians. They wore face paint, blankets, and feathers. They got on the ships. They picked up the tea chests. They used hammers, knives, and shovels to smash the chests. They then dumped the tea into the water. As they left, they chanted, "Tell King George we'll pay no taxes on his tea!"

Error Summary	
Capitalization	6
Punctuation:	
Apostrophe	1
Comma	5
Period	1
Quotation Mark	1
Other	1
Spelling	1

WEDNESDAY — WEEK 23

King George was ~~angerie~~ angry about the tea. He closed the harbor, outlawed meetings, and put soldiers in the city. He thought the colonists would give in.

"This means war!" shouted the colonists. "We will rule ourselves from now on!" The colonists won the war. There wouldn't be a king. They would vote for laws and taxes.

Error Summary	
Capitalization	4
Punctuation:	
Apostrophe	1
Comma	2
Period	1
Quotation Mark	3
Other	2
Spelling	1

THURSDAY — WEEK 23

Name ____

A groope of men dressed up like Indians. They wore face paint blankets and feathers. They got on the ships they picked up the tea chests. They used hammers knives and shovels to smash the chests. they then dumped the tea into the water. as they left, they chanted tell king george wel'l pay no taxes on his tea."

WATCH FOR

- dialog
- commas
- exclamations

WEDNESDAY **WEEK 23**

King George was angerie about the tea. he closed the harbor outlawed meetings and put soldiers in the city. He thought the colonists would give in.

this means war" shouted the colonists. We will rule ourselves from now on. the colonists won the war. There wouldnt be a king they would vote for laws and taxes.

WATCH FOR

- dialog
- commas
- exclamations

THURSDAY **WEEK 23**

Preview the 4 daily lessons to ensure you review or introduce skills that may be unfamiliar to students.

Letters Home

Dear tilly

I got to new york city new york, one-half month ago. It was a tiring lonely ride over on the ship, the SS Ford. I was seasick for about one third of the voyage. For the first week, I stayed at 64 E ninth St I miss you but I like this friendly exciting country. You will join me soon

Error Summary	
Capitalization	7
Punctuation:	
Comma	5
Period	3
Other	2

MONDAY WEEK 24

I met a man named nick in new york. Thanks to him, I got a job at a steel mill in pittsburgh pennsylvania. It took one half of my money for the train ticket but I got there I stayed at 112 N oak Ave with nick

Your loving Husband

anders

Error Summary	
Capitalization	9
Punctuation:	
Comma	3
Period	4
Other	1

TUESDAY WEEK 24

Name ______________________________

Letters Home

Dear tilly

I got to new york city new york, one-half month ago. It was a tiring lonely ride over on the ship, the SS Ford. I was seasick for about one third of the voyage. For the first week, I stayed at 64 E ninth St I miss you but I like this friendly exciting country. You will join me soon

WATCH FOR

- names of places and ships
- hyphens

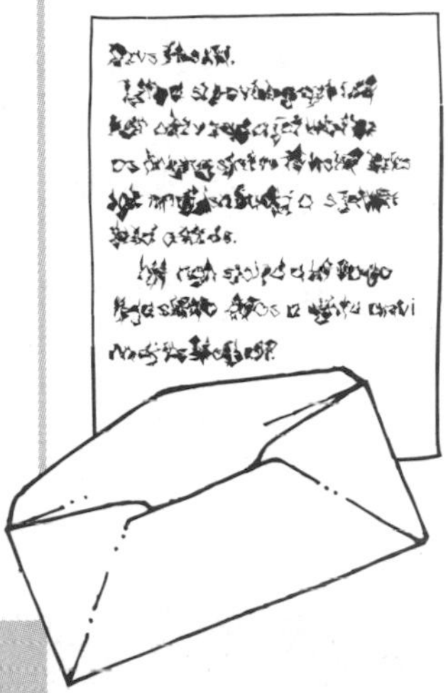

MONDAY **WEEK 24**

I met a man named nick in new york. Thanks to him, I got a job at a steel mill in pittsburgh pennsylvania. It took one half of my money for the train ticket but I got there I stayed at 112 N oak Ave with nick

Your loving Husband

anders

WATCH FOR

- names of places
- hyphens

TUESDAY **WEEK 24**

Dear tilly,

I have a new job on a large ship. It is named the USS Traveler. I shovel cole coal, and I keep the ship's powerful, hungry engines running. It was a busy, hard trip from new york to san francisco, california. I worrk work for two-thirds of each day. After work, I ride cable cars on hyde St. and powell St.

Error Summary	
Capitalization	8
Punctuation:	
Comma	5
Period	5
Other	1
Spelling	2

WEDNESDAY **WEEK 24**

I will send for you in three-fourths of a year. You can take the ship, the SS Hanson, to new york city. The "USS Traveler" will be there, and we will take it to portland, oregon. I bought a farm there on maple Rd. for us.

Your Loving husband,

anders

Error Summary	
Capitalization	8
Punctuation:	
Comma	4
Period	2
Quotation Mark	2
Other	3

THURSDAY **WEEK 24**

Name ____________________________________

Dear tilly

I have a new job on a large ship It is named the USS Traveler. I shovel cole and I keep the ship's powerful hungry engines running It was a busy hard trip from new york to san francisco california. I worrk for two thirds of each day After work, I ride cable cars on hyde St and powell St

WATCH FOR

- names of places and ships
- hyphens

WEDNESDAY **WEEK 24**

I will send for you in three fourths of a year. You can take the ship, the SS Hanson to new york city. The "USS Traveler" will be there and we will take it to portland oregon. I bought a farm there on maple Rd for us

Your Loving husband

anders

WATCH FOR

- names of places and ships
- hyphens

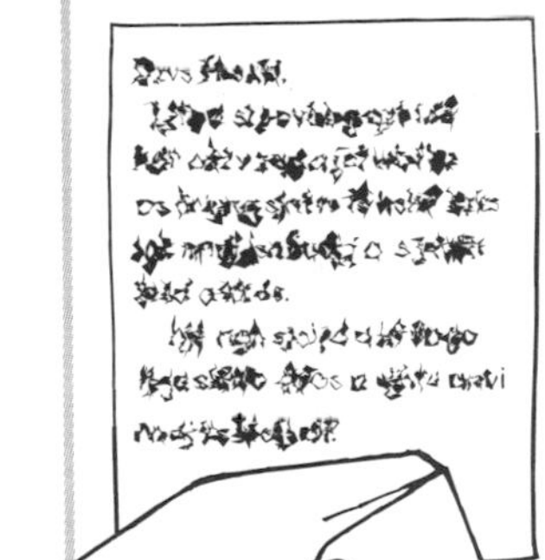

THURSDAY **WEEK 24**

Preview the 4 daily lessons to ensure you review or introduce skills that may be unfamiliar to students.

The Boy Who Cried Wolf

Long ~~ugo~~ ago, there was a young shepherd boy. He ~~tooked~~ took care of the sheep. He made ~~shure~~ sure they ~~was~~ were safe and didn't wander off alone. The job was boring, so the boy played a trick on the village people. He stood on a tree stump and yelled, "Wolf! Wolf! A wolf is after the sheep!"

Error Summary

Language Usage	2
Punctuation:	
Apostrophe	1
Comma	1
Quotation Mark	1
Other	1
Spelling	2

MONDAY — **WEEK 25**

The villagers ~~grabed~~ grabbed rakes and sticks. They ran to the hillside. The boy laughed at them and said, "Silly villagers! There ~~are~~ is no wolf. It's a joke I made up."

The villagers didn't think it was funny. "Don't play tricks on us!" one man said. The villagers then went back to their work.

Error Summary

Language Usage	1
Punctuation:	
Apostrophe	3
Period	1
Quotation Mark	2
Other	2
Spelling	1

TUESDAY — **WEEK 25**

Name ______________________________

The Boy Who Cried Wolf

Long ugo, there was a young shepherd boy. He tooked care of the sheep. He made shure they was safe and didnt wander off alone. The job was boring, so the boy played a trick on the village people. He stood on a tree stump and yelled "Wolf! Wolf A wolf is after the sheep!

WATCH FOR

- dialog
- exclamations

MONDAY **WEEK 25**

The villagers grabed rakes and sticks. They ran to the hillside The boy laughed at them and said, Silly villagers There are no wolf. Its a joke I made up."

The villagers didnt think it was funny. Dont play tricks on us" one man said. The villagers then went back to their work.

WATCH FOR

- dialog
- exclamations

TUESDAY **WEEK 25**

A few days later, the boy ~~were~~ was bored again. He wondered if his trick would work ~~wonce~~ once more. The boy ~~standed~~ stood on the stump and cried, "Wolf! Wolf! I need help!"

Again the ~~villagirs~~ villagers ran to help the boy. "Ha, ha! I fooled you!" laughed the shepherd boy.

"We're angry about your mean tricks," they told him.

Error Summary

Language Usage	2
Punctuation:	
Apostrophe	1
Comma	1
Quotation Mark	2
Other	2
Spelling	2

WEDNESDAY **WEEK 25**

The next day ~~begane~~ began peacefully. Then a wolf really did attack the ~~sheap~~ sheep. The boy jumped onto the stump and yelled, "A wolf ~~are~~ is killing the sheep~~?~~! I mean it!"

"I won't be fooled again," said one villager.

"Neither will we," said the others. They all went back ~~two~~ to work. The poor shepherd boy watched the wolf ~~eats~~ eat his sheep.

Error Summary

Language Usage	2
Punctuation:	
Apostrophe	1
Comma	1
Period	1
Quotation Mark	3
Other	2
Spelling	3

THURSDAY **WEEK 25**

Name ________________________________

A few days later, the boy were bored again. He wondered if his trick would work wonce more. The boy standed on the stump and cried “Wolf Wolf! I need help!

Again the villagirs ran to help the boy. “Ha, ha! I fooled you” laughed the shepherd boy.

“Were angry about your mean tricks, they told him.

WATCH FOR

- dialog
- exclamations

WEDNESDAY **WEEK 25**

The next day begane peacefully. Then a wolf really did attack the sheap. The boy jumped onto the stump and yelled, “A wolf are killing the sheep? I mean it

“I wont be fooled again, said one villager.

Neither will we” said the others. They all went back two work. The poor shepherd boy watched the wolf eats his sheep

WATCH FOR

- dialog
- exclamations

THURSDAY **WEEK 25**

Preview the 4 daily lessons to ensure you review or introduce skills that may be unfamiliar to students.

Welcome to the Arctic Tundra

The arctic tundra is the coldest and driest ~~dryest~~ biome. It's around the north pole. There are also tundra areas in europe, asia, and North america. There's about one-half foot of rain there each year. The growing season is one-sixth of a year long. The temperature is below ~~beloe~~ 32 degrees for about ten-twelfths of the year.

Error Summary	
Capitalization	6
Punctuation:	
Apostrophe	2
Comma	2
Period	3
Other	2
Spelling	2

MONDAY WEEK 26

About 1,700 kinds of plants grow in the tundra. One-fourth of the plants have flowers. The other three-fourths of the plants are shrubs, mosses, sedges, and grasses. Their roots can't go very deep. A layer of permafrost is one-half foot below the surface. The frozen ground won't let water get into the soil below it.

Error Summary	
Punctuation:	
Apostrophe	2
Comma	3
Period	4
Other	3

TUESDAY WEEK 26

Name ______________________________

Welcome to the Arctic Tundra

The arctic tundra is the coldest and dryest biome I'ts around the north pole. There are also tundra areas in europe asia and North america. Theres about one-half foot of rain there each year The growing season is one sixth of a year long. The temperature is beloe 32 degrees for about ten twelfths of the year

WATCH FOR

- names of places
- commas
- hyphens

MONDAY **WEEK 26**

About 1,700 kinds of plants grow in the tundra One fourth of the plants have flowers The other three fourths of the plants are shrubs mosses sedges and grasses. Their roots cant go very deep A layer of permafrost is one half foot below the surface. The frozen ground wont let water get into the soil below it

WATCH FOR

- commas
- hyphens

TUESDAY **WEEK 26**

eating
Plant-eoting animals such as caribou, hares, and squirrels live in the tundra. The foxes, wolves, and polar bears eat meat. Arctic animals have short bodies, extra fat, and thick fur. They don't get too cold. Most of the animals sleep all winter. The caribou live in canada, greenland, and alaska.

Error Summary

Capitalization	3
Punctuation:	
Apostrophe	1
Comma	8
Period	3
Spelling	1

WEDNESDAY **WEEK 26**

Ravens, falcons, loons, and snowbirds live in the tundra. These birds don't always stay there. They fly south for the winter. Some fly to canada. The snowy owls fly all the way to virginia. There aren't many snakes, lizards, or frogs. The weather wether isn't warm enough for them. Cod, trout, salmon, and other fish live in the cold waters.

Error Summary

Capitalization	2
Punctuation:	
Apostrophe	3
Comma	8
Period	4
Spelling	1

THURSDAY **WEEK 26**

Name ______________________________

Plant-eeting animals such as caribou hares and squirrels live in the tundra The foxes wolves and polar bears eat meat. Arctic animals have short bodies extra fat and thick fur. They dont get too cold. Most of the animals sleep all winter The caribou live in canada greenland and alaska

WATCH FOR

- names of places
- commas

WEDNESDAY **WEEK 26**

Ravens falcons loons and snowbirds live in the tundra These birds dont always stay there They fly south for the winter. Some fly to canada. The snowy owls fly all the way to virginia. There arent many snakes lizards or frogs. The wether isnt warm enough for them Cod trout salmon and other fish live in the cold waters

WATCH FOR

- names of places
- commas

THURSDAY **WEEK 26**

Preview the 4 daily lessons to ensure you review or introduce skills that may be unfamiliar to students.

Liak, an Inuit Girl

my name is Liak. I am Inuit (IN-oo-it). The inuit are people who live in the cold arctic lands in alaska, canada, and greenland. I live with mom, dad, and my brothers. Mom's name is noayak. Dad's ~~names~~ name is baral. My brothers' names are qayak and tuma. our family, And friends have always lived here.

Error Summary

Capitalization	14
Language Usage	1
Punctuation:	
Apostrophe	3
Comma	4
Period	2

MONDAY **WEEK 27**

winter here is long, dark, and very cold. It lasts from october until march. My family and I wear ~~his~~ our warm parkas, watertight boots, and thick ~~glove~~ gloves. I like the summer, especially july and august. we have sunshine all day and night. my friends and I play outside a lot. Mom's flower garden is beautiful.

Error Summary

Capitalization	7
Language Usage	2
Punctuation:	
Apostrophe	1
Comma	4
Period	2

TUESDAY **WEEK 27**

Name ________________________________

Liak, an Inuit Girl

my name is Liak. I am Inuit (IN-oo-it). The inuit are people who live in the cold arctic lands in alaska canada and greenland. I live with mom dad and my brothers. Moms name is noayak. Dads names is baral. My brothers names are qayak and tuma. our family. And friends have always lived here

WATCH FOR

- names of people and places
- commas

MONDAY **WEEK 27**

winter here is long dark and very cold. It lasts from october until march. My family and I wear his warm parkas watertight boots and thick glove. I like the summer, especially july and august. we have sunshine all day and night my friends and I play outside a lot. Moms flower garden is beautiful

WATCH FOR

- commas

TUESDAY **WEEK 27**

my ancestors homes ~~was~~ were huts or tents they traveled By ~~foots~~ foot, dogsled or boat. They hunted whales seals and walruses. I have an easier life my ~~families~~ family's house is modern We use snowmobiles cars airplanes and motorboats. mom and dad buy our food at a big store. I buy clothes CDs and video games there, too

Error Summary	
Capitalization	6
Language Usage	2
Punctuation:	
Apostrophe	1
Comma	8
Period	4
Spelling	1

WEDNESDAY **WEEK 27**

mom and dad are ~~teacher~~ teachers. my two ~~brother~~ brothers and I go to school We learn math reading science English and our native language. qayak makes inuit carvings. he sells them in many stores at craft fairs and on the Internet. Tumas ~~hobbies~~ hobby is playing the guitar I like to teach the old Inuit ~~storys~~ stories, legends and songs to others

Error Summary	
Capitalization	6
Language Usage	3
Punctuation:	
Apostrophe	1
Comma	7
Period	3
Spelling	1

THURSDAY **WEEK 27**

Name ______________________________

my ancestors homes was huts or tents they traveled By foots, dogsled or boat. They hunted whales seals and walruses. I have an easier life my families house is modern We use snowmobiles cars airplanes and motorboats. mom and dad buy our food at a big store. I buy clothes CDs and video games there, too

WATCH FOR

• commas

WEDNESDAY **WEEK 27**

mom and dad are teacher. my two brother and I go to school We learn math reading science English and our native language. qayak makes inuit carvings. he sells them in many stores at craft fairs and on the Internet. Tumas' hobbies is playing the guitar I like to teach the old Inuit storys, legends and songs to others

WATCH FOR

• commas

THURSDAY **WEEK 27**

Preview the 4 daily lessons to ensure you review or introduce skills that may be unfamiliar to students.

The Dog Ate My Homework

It was a bright sunny saturday. The phone rang, and I ~~ansered~~ answered. My friend, tina, was on the line.

Tina said "can you go to the recreation center, kendra sally, keesha, and ~~me~~ I are going

I moaned and said I cant. Im on restriction Heres my story.

Error Summary	
Capitalization	6
Language Usage	1
Punctuation:	
Apostrophe	3
Comma	3
Quotation Mark	3
Other	1
Spelling	1

MONDAY **WEEK 28**

On tuesday, mr. hobson said Wheres your homework, kendra johnson Please give ~~him~~ it to me

I replied, my silly hungry dog ate it

On wednesday, Mr hobson said where is ~~you~~ your homework, Kendra! Did you ~~ferget~~ forget it?

"I said," my mean cranky brother matt tore it

Error Summary	
Capitalization	11
Language Usage	2
Punctuation:	
Apostrophe	1
Comma	6
Period	1
Quotation Mark	10
Other	2
Spelling	1

TUESDAY **WEEK 28**

Name ______________________________

The Dog Ate My Homework

It was a bright sunny saturday. The phone rang, and I anserd. My friend, tina, was on the line.

Tina said "can you go to the recreation center, kendra. sally, keesha, and me are going.

I moaned and said I cant. Im on restriction. Heres my story.

WATCH FOR

- commas
- questions
- dialog

MONDAY **WEEK 28**

On tuesday, mr. hobson said Wheres' your homework, kendra johnson. Please give him to me.

I replied, my silly hungry dog ate it.

On wednesday, Mr hobson said where is you homework, Kendra! Did you ferget it?

"I said," my mean cranky brother matt tore it.

WATCH FOR

- commas
- questions
- dialog

TUESDAY **WEEK 28**

On thursday, Mr hobson asked, do you have your homework? did you bring it today?"

I told him, no, it went down the kitchen sink. Ms reston, the young new plumber, couldnt get it out.

mr. Hobson asked me again on friday. I answered I was too feverish to work. I needed to relax.

Error Summary

Capitalization	8
Punctuation:	
Apostrophe	1
Comma	2
Period	2
Quotation Mark	5
Other	1

WEDNESDAY **WEEK 28**

mr. hobson called my mom. He said "Mrs johnson, kendra hasnt turned in her homework all week.

He put me on the telephone. "Mom said why didnt you do your work? thats a careless, irresponsible way to behave. youll finish it on saturday and sunday.

I learned my lesson I wont skip homework ever again!

Error Summary

Capitalization	9
Punctuation:	
Apostrophe	5
Comma	2
Period	2
Quotation Mark	4
Other	1

THURSDAY **WEEK 28**

Name ______________________________

On thursday, Mr hobson asked, do you have your homework, did you bring it today?"

I told him, no, it went down the kitchen sink. Ms reston, the young new plumber, couldnt get it out.

mr. Hobson asked me again on friday. I answered I was too feverish to work. I needed to relax.

WATCH FOR

- commas
- questions
- dialog

WEDNESDAY **WEEK 28**

mr. hobson called my mom. He said "Mrs johnson, kendra hasnt turned in her homework all week.

He put me on the telephone. "Mom said why didnt you do your work thats a careless, irresponsible way to behave. youll finish it on saturday and sunday.

I learned my lesson I wont skip homework ever again!

WATCH FOR

- commas
- questions
- dialog

THURSDAY **WEEK 28**

Preview the 4 daily lessons to ensure you review or introduce skills that may be unfamiliar to students.

A Holiday Diary

december 25 2003

dear diary

Its christmas day I have a new diary Im so excited! I can't wait to write ~~right~~ every day. Ill tell about things that happen. I will also draw some pictures Theyl'l go with the words I want to be an author and illustrator when i grow up. this diary will be a good place to practice

Error Summary	
Capitalization	7
Punctuation:	
Apostrophe	5
Comma	3
Period	5
Spelling	1

MONDAY WEEK 29

december 26. 2003

dear diary

Hooray! today is the first day of kwanzaa Our family celebrates it after christmas. it lasts for seven days. dad said that this holiday started in America in 1966 Each day, we talk about ways to make our lives better we also light a candle

Error Summary	
Capitalization	9
Punctuation:	
Comma	2
Period	4
Other	1

TUESDAY WEEK 29

Name ______________________________

A Holiday Diary

december, 25 2003

dear diary

Its christmas day I have a new diary Im so excited! I cant wait to right every day. Ill tell about things that happen. I will also draw some pictures Theyl'l go with the words I want to be an author and illustrator when i grow up. this diary will be a good place to practice

WATCH FOR

- dates
- salutations
- holidays

MONDAY **WEEK 29**

december 26. 2003

dear diary

Hooray today is the first day of kwanzaa Our family celebrates it after christmas. it lasts for seven days. dad said that this holiday started in America in 1966 Each day, we talk about ways to make our lives better we also light a candle

WATCH FOR

- dates
- salutations
- holidays
- exclamations

TUESDAY **WEEK 29**

december 31 2003

dear diary

Its the sixth day of kwanzaa we spent the past four for days at grandma and grandpa's house We all had a fun time. each evening, we celebrated together. We lit the candles ate lots of good food and listened to music from Africa. I didnt have time to write in my diary

Error Summary

Capitalization	8
Punctuation:	
Apostrophe	2
Comma	4
Period	3
Spelling	1

WEDNESDAY **WEEK 29**

january 1 2004

dear diary

Wow! today is the last day of kwanzaa It's a day to celebrate faith. mom says that faith is believing that good things will happen Also, today is new year's day. I have one new year's resolution. I will write in my diary every week, thats a promise!

Error Summary

Capitalization	12
Punctuation:	
Apostrophe	2
Comma	2
Period	3
Other	2

THURSDAY **WEEK 29**

Name ______________________

december 31 2003

dear diary.

Its the sixth day of kwanzaa we spent the past for days at grandma and grandpa's house We all had a fun time. each evening, we celebrated together. We lit the candles ate lots of good food and listened to music from Africa. I didnt have time to write in my diary

WATCH FOR

- dates
- salutations
- holidays

WEDNESDAY **WEEK 29**

january 1 2004

dear diary

Wow today is the last day of kwanzaa Its a day to celebrate faith. mom says that faith is believing that good things will happen Also, today is new year's day. I have one new year's resolution. I will write in my diary every week, thats a promise

WATCH FOR

- dates
- salutations
- holidays
- exclamations

THURSDAY **WEEK 29**

Preview the 4 daily lessons to ensure you review or introduce skills that may be unfamiliar to students.

Who Ya Gonna Call? Robot Helpers!

Who does work that people don't do? Robots, that's who Robots are machines that have computers inside them they can move. They have sensors that let them see hear and touch things. People program ~~robbots~~ robots. the robots then do their jobs. Robots drill holes spray paint and put together cars. Wow! thats a lot of work, !

Error Summary	
Capitalization	3
Punctuation:	
Apostrophe	1
Comma	4
Period	2
Other	1
Spelling	1

MONDAY WEEK 30

Do robots help with disasters? Yes, they sure do There was an accident in a nuclear power plant the building wasnt safe for people. A robot went in cleaned up the mess and came out safely.

Have you ever seen a fallen building? Robots can look through the rubble find victims and signal rescuers

Error Summary	
Capitalization	1
Punctuation:	
Apostrophe	1
Comma	4
Period	3
Other	1

TUESDAY WEEK 30

Name ______________________________

Who Ya Gonna Call? Robot Helpers!

Who does work that people don't do? Robots, that's who Robots are machines that have computers inside them they can move. They have sensors that let them see hear and touch things. People program robbots. the robots then do their jobs. Robots drill holes spray paint and put together cars. Wow! thats a lot of work.

WATCH FOR

- commas
- exclamations

MONDAY **WEEK 30**

Do robots help with disasters? Yes, they sure do There was an accident in a nuclear power plant the building wasnt safe for people. A robot went in cleaned up the mess and came out safely.

Have you ever seen a fallen building Robots can look through the rubble find victims and signal rescuers

WATCH FOR

- commas
- questions

TUESDAY **WEEK 30**

How do robots help the space program? Astronauts couldn't go to Mars, but a robot did. It collected rocks, read temperatures, and took pictures. A robot camera is now looking for life on other planets. It takes pictures, records information, and sends it all back to the scientists. Goodness! that's a big job!

Error Summary	
Capitalization	1
Punctuation:	
Apostrophe	1
Comma	4
Period	2
Other	2

WEDNESDAY **WEEK 30**

What other hard tasks can robots do? robots go where people can't go. They crawl into volcanoes, take samples of gases, and examine the smoke. Robots dive deep in the oceans, look at strange creatures, and record temperatures. Gee! that's dangerous! Aren't you glad we have robots?

Error Summary	
Capitalization	2
Punctuation:	
Apostrophe	3
Comma	4
Period	1
Other	3

THURSDAY **WEEK 30**

Name ______________________________

How do robots help the space program? Astronauts couldn't go to Mars, but a robot did It collected rocks read temperatures and took pictures. A robot camera is now looking for life on other planets It takes pictures records information and sends it all back to the scientists. Goodness thats a big job

WATCH FOR

- commas
- exclamations

WEDNESDAY **WEEK 30**

What other hard tasks can robots do? robots go where people cant go. They crawl into volcanoes take samples of gases and examine the smoke Robots dive deep in the oceans look at strange creatures and record temperatures. Gee thats dangerous Arent you glad we have robots

WATCH FOR

- commas
- exclamations
- questions

THURSDAY **WEEK 30**

Preview the 4 daily lessons to ensure you review or introduce skills that may be unfamiliar to students.

The History of Calendars

Long, long ago, people made the first calendars, To keep track of the seasons These ~~calinders~~ calendars divided the year by the moons cycles. There ~~were~~ was a full moon about 12 times between one spring and the next and there were 29 or 30 days between each full moon. The year was divided into 12 lunar months it had 354 days

Error Summary

Capitalization	2
Language Usage	1
Punctuation:	
Apostrophe	1
Comma	1
Period	4
Spelling	1

MONDAY WEEK 31

The people of babylon used the lunar calendar but They didnt ~~no~~ know that there were really 365 days in a year. Their lunar calendar was 11 days short each year After a few years, the seasons and ~~munths~~ months didnt match up. Every eight years, three months had to be added The Babylonians got very mixed up!

Error Summary

Capitalization	2
Punctuation:	
Apostrophe	2
Comma	1
Period	2
Spelling	2

TUESDAY WEEK 31

Name ______________________________

The History of Calendars

Long, long ago, people made the first calendars. To keep track of the seasons These calinders divided the year by the moons cycles. There were a full moon about 12 times between one spring and the next and there were 29 or 30 days between each full moon. The year was divided into 12 lunar months it had 354 days

WATCH FOR

- commas

MONDAY **WEEK 31**

The people of babylon used the lunar calendar but They didnt no that there were really 365 days in a year. Their lunar calendar was 11 days short each year After a few years, the seasons and munths didnt match up. Every eight years, three months had to be added The Babylonians got very mixed up!

WATCH FOR

- commas

TUESDAY **WEEK 31**

The egyptians looked at the stars in the sky They saw that the Dog Star rose next to the sun every 365 days. They made a calendar and they based it on the sun. This calendar Divided the 365 days into 12 ~~month~~ months. This worked well Weve based our ~~calender~~ calendar on the one from ancient egypt.

Error Summary

Capitalization	3
Language Usage	1
Punctuation:	
Apostrophe	1
Comma	1
Period	2
Spelling	1

WEDNESDAY **WEEK 31**

An emperor in rome made another calendar with 12 months of 30 or 31 days each He ~~aded~~ added a leap year with 80 extra days every four years but this was too confusing.

In 1582, a math ~~experts~~ expert changed the Rules for leap year and made the calendar more exact. The ~~season~~ seasons didnt move around anymore. We use this calendar today

Error Summary

Capitalization	2
Language Usage	2
Punctuation:	
Apostrophe	1
Comma	1
Period	2
Spelling	1

THURSDAY **WEEK 31**

Name ______________________________

The egyptians looked at the stars in the sky They saw that the Dog Star rose next to the sun every 365 days. They made a calendar and they based it on the sun. This calendar Divided the 365 days into 12 month. This worked well Weve based our calender on the one from ancient egypt.

WATCH FOR

- commas

WEDNESDAY **WEEK 31**

An emperor in rome made another calendar with 12 months of 30 or 31 days each He aded a leap year with 80 extra days every four years but this was too confusing.

In 1582, a math experts changed the Rules for leap year and made the calendar more exact. The season didnt move around anymore. We use this calendar today

WATCH FOR

- commas

THURSDAY **WEEK 31**

Preview the 4 daily lessons to ensure you review or introduce skills that may be unfamiliar to students.

Shadows

do you know what makes a shadow? First, some light is necessary Next, there has to be something ~~blokking~~ blocking the light. When you are ~~outsied~~ outside during the day, bright light comes from the sun. if you block the sunlight a shadow will appear on the opposite side of you

Error Summary	
Capitalization	2
Punctuation:	
Comma	1
Period	2
Other	1
Spelling	2

MONDAY **WEEK 32**

have you seen your shadow at several different times of the day? What did the size and shape look like? The size and ~~shap~~ shape depend on the sun's location in the sky. if the sun is directly overhead a shadow will be short and fat. if the sun is lower in the sky a shadow will be long and skinny

Error Summary	
Capitalization	3
Punctuation:	
Comma	2
Period	1
Other	1
Spelling	1

TUESDAY **WEEK 32**

Name ____________________

Shadows

do you know what makes a shadow First, some light is necessary Next, there has to be something blokking the light. When you are outsied during the day, bright light comes from the sun. if you block the sunlight a shadow will appear on the opposite side of you

WATCH FOR

- questions
- commas

MONDAY **WEEK 32**

have you seen your shadow at several different times of the day? What did the size and shape look like The size and shap depend on the sun's location in the sky. if the sun is directly overhead a shadow will be short and fat. if the sun is lower in the sky a shadow will be long and skinny

WATCH FOR

- questions
- commas

TUESDAY **WEEK 32**

have you ever been frightened by unusual shadows in your bedroom at night? what do you discover if you turn on more lights? Anything that blocks light can create a scary shadow on your wall. Shadows are visible even after dark. there has to be a small amount of light shining ~~threw~~ through a window to make a shadow.

Error Summary

Capitalization	3
Punctuation:	
Period	2
Other	1
Spelling	1

WEDNESDAY **WEEK 32**

you can have a great time with shadows. Shine a flashlight on a small object. look past the object and you will see its shadow. have you ever played shadow tag? ~~Wate~~ Wait for a sunny day, and then go outside with friends. The person who is "It" tries to step on the other players' shadows. Playing shadow tag is fun.

Error Summary

Capitalization	3
Punctuation:	
Apostrophe	1
Comma	1
Period	4
Other	1
Spelling	1

THURSDAY **WEEK 32**

Name ______________________________

have you ever been frightened by unusual shadows in your bedroom at night? what do you discover if you turn on more lights Anything that blocks light can create a scary shadow on your wall Shadows are visible even after dark. there has to be a small amount of light shining threw a window to make a shadow

WATCH FOR

- questions

WEDNESDAY **WEEK 32**

you can have a great time with shadows. Shine a flashlight on a small object look past the object and you will see its shadow have you ever played shadow tag Wate for a sunny day and then go outside with friends. The person who is “It” tries to step on the other players shadows Playing shadow tag is fun

WATCH FOR

- questions
- commas

THURSDAY **WEEK 32**

Preview the 4 daily lessons to ensure you review or introduce skills that may be unfamiliar to students.

The Ups and Downs of Roller Coasters

when it comes to speedy roller coasters, gravity rules ~~rooles~~! From the very beginning, roller coasters have worked by a simple ~~simply~~ scientific rule: What goes up must come down. Gravity makes that happen ~~happin~~. Gravity is a natural force. It makes objects move toward Earth's center.

Error Summary	
Capitalization	1
Language Usage	1
Punctuation:	
Apostrophe	1
Comma	1
Period	2
Spelling	2

MONDAY WEEK 33

the first hill of a roller coaster ride has to be the steepest. gravity quickly pulls the coaster down that hill. It creates enough energy. For the ride to coast ~~coste~~ easily along until it comes to another hill. no hill can be higher than the first. It would take more energy to go up the rest of the hills than the cars had at the start.

Error Summary	
Capitalization	4
Punctuation:	
Period	3
Spelling	1

TUESDAY WEEK 33

Name ____________________________________

The Ups and Downs of Roller Coasters

when it comes to speedy roller coasters, gravity rooles! From the very beginning roller coasters have worked by a simply scientific rule: What goes up must come down Gravity makes that happin. Gravity is a natural force. It makes objects move toward Earths center

WATCH FOR

- commas

MONDAY **WEEK 33**

the first hill of a roller coaster ride has to be the steepest gravity quickly pulls the coaster down that hill. It creates enough energy. For the ride to coste easily along until it comes to another hill. no hill can be higher than the first. It would take more energy to go up the rest of the hills than the cars had at the start

TUESDAY **WEEK 33**

rapidly around

as coasters fly ~~rapid~~ down hills and ~~arownd~~ curves, they create G-forces. A G-force is the heavy pressure riders feel. The original roller coasters were circular. they created very strong G-forces. The forces were too hard on people. some got sick. later, tracks in teardrop shapes were tried. They did not cause such powerful G-forces.

Error Summary

Capitalization	4
Language Usage	1
Punctuation:	
Comma	1
Period	3
Spelling	1

WEDNESDAY **WEEK 33**

Today, roller coasters speed down steep hills up to 94.48 meters (310 ft) tall. they hit speeds of up to 100 miles per hour, and they may loop up to eight times. rides may be short or long. One-half minute (30 sec) is about the shortest. the longest, so far, is 90 seconds ($1\frac{1}{2}$ min). Gravity makes all of these great rides possible.

Error Summary

Capitalization	3
Punctuation:	
Comma	1
Period	5

THURSDAY **WEEK 33**

Name ______________________________

as coasters fly rapid down hills and arownd curves they create G-forces. A G-force is the heavy pressure riders feel. The original roller coasters were circular they created very strong G-forces. The forces were too hard on people, some got sick. later, tracks in teardrop shapes were tried. They did not cause such powerful G-forces

WATCH FOR

- commas

WEDNESDAY **WEEK 33**

Today, roller coasters speed down steep hills up to 94.48 meters (310 ft) tall. they hit speeds of up to 100 miles per hour and they may loop up to eight times. rides may be short or long. One-half minute (30 sec) is about the shortest. the longest, so far, is 90 seconds ($1\frac{1}{2}$ min) Gravity makes all of these great rides possible

WATCH FOR

- commas
- abbreviations

THURSDAY **WEEK 33**

Preview the 4 daily lessons to ensure you review or introduce skills that may be unfamiliar to students.

The First Computer Bug

On september 9, 1945, I was at harvard university to test a ~~knew~~ new computer program for the Mark II Calculator.

I said, "Something isn't right here, Dan."

Dan, my co-worker, said, "What's that, Max?"

I said, "The program was supposed to ~~ad~~ add, but it subtracted. It was supposed to multiply, but it divided."

Error Summary	
Capitalization	3
Punctuation:	
Apostrophe	1
Comma	4
Quotation Mark	3
Spelling	2

MONDAY WEEK 34

We ~~herd~~ heard crackling sounds, and we saw sparks. The computer wasn't working at all. I took off the machine's glass cover. I said, "there's a two-inch-long moth, Dan. It's stuck between points at Relay 70, Panel F."

Dan said, "max, you found a bug in the computer?"

I said, "Yes, Dan. I think it caused our problems."

Error Summary	
Capitalization	2
Punctuation:	
Apostrophe	1
Comma	7
Period	1
Quotation Mark	6
Spelling	1

TUESDAY WEEK 34

Name ______________________________

The First Computer Bug

On september 9 1945, I was at harvard university to test a knew computer program for the Mark II Calculator.

I said, "Something isnt right here, Dan.

Dan, my co-worker, said "What's that Max?

I said, "The program was supposed to ad, but it subtracted. It was supposed to multiply but it divided.

WATCH FOR

- dialog
- commas

MONDAY **WEEK 34**

We herd crackling sounds and we saw sparks. The computer wasn't working at all. I took off the machines' glass cover. I said there's a two-inch-long moth Dan. It's stuck between points at Relay 70, Panel F.

Dan said max you found a bug in the computer?

I said Yes Dan. I think it caused our problems

WATCH FOR

- dialog
- commas

TUESDAY **WEEK 34**

I removed the moth, and then I put the computer's cover back on. Dan started the Mark II, and it worked!

I taped the bug to the day's log page. I ~~rote~~ wrote, "First actual case of bug being found. september 9, 1945."

We told Hopper, our boss, the ~~hole~~ whole story. Dan said, "we debugged the computer, Hopper."

Error Summary

Capitalization	2
Punctuation:	
Apostrophe	2
Comma	6
Quotation Mark	3
Spelling	2

WEDNESDAY — WEEK 34

Hopper said, "guys, we just made history!" soon, every computer problem was called a "bug".

On september 9, 1999, I was at the smithsonian Institution with Dan. We saw a logbook. The book's ink hadn't faded, and the moth was still taped there.

Dan said, "max, there's our computer bug!"

Error Summary

Capitalization	5
Punctuation:	
Apostrophe	1
Comma	5
Period	1
Quotation Mark	4

THURSDAY — WEEK 34

Name ______________________________

I removed the moth and then I put the computers cover back on. Dan started the Mark II and it worked!

I taped the bug to the days log page. I rote First actual case of bug being found. september 9 1945."

We told Hopper, our boss, the hole story.

Dan said we debugged the computer Hopper.

WATCH FOR

- dialog
- commas

WEDNESDAY **WEEK 34**

Hopper said, guys we just made history! soon, every computer problem was called a "bug"

On september 9 1999, I was at the smithsonian Institution with Dan. We saw a logbook. The books ink hadn't faded and the moth was still taped there.

Dan said max there's our computer bug!

WATCH FOR

- dialog
- commas

THURSDAY **WEEK 34**

Preview the 4 daily lessons to ensure you review or introduce skills that may be unfamiliar to students.

Cactus—A Desert Plant

Cactuses grow in hot, dry deserts. The smallest cactus is about 5 centimeters (2 in.) tall. The largest cactus is about 18 meters (60 ft.) tall. All cactuses can store water. the water is gathered by roots, and then the plant stores it. The roots usually grow down 2.5 centimeters (1 in.) to 15 centimeters (6 in.) deep in the soil. they absorb water quickly.

Error Summary	
Capitalization	2
Punctuation:	
Comma	2
Period	4

MONDAY WEEK 35

A cholla cactus has sharp, prickly spines. The spines come off ~~easy~~ easily. Chollas vary in size from 10 centimeters (4 in.) to 3 meters (10 ft.) tall. Some of their ~~flours~~ flowers are 4 centimeters (1½ in.) wide. pack rats collect the stems and then pile them up in front of their burrows. the stems protect the pack rats from their dangerous, hungry enemies.

Error Summary	
Capitalization	2
Language Usage	1
Punctuation:	
Comma	2
Period	3
Spelling	1

TUESDAY WEEK 35

Name ______________________

Cactus—A Desert Plant

Cactuses grow in hot dry deserts. The smallest cactus is about 5 centimeters (2 in) tall. The largest cactus is about 18 meters (60 ft) tall. All cactuses can store water. the water is gathered by roots and then the plant stores it. The roots usually grow down 2.5 centimeters (1 in) to 15 centimeters (6 in) deep in the soil. they absorb water quickly.

WATCH FOR

- commas
- abbreviations

MONDAY **WEEK 35**

A cholla cactus has sharp prickly spines. The spines come off easy. Chollas vary in size from 10 centimeters (4 in) to 3 meters (10 ft) tall. Some of their flours are 4 centimeters ($1\frac{1}{2}$ in) wide. pack rats collect the stems and then pile them up in front of their burrows. the stems protect the pack rats from their dangerous hungry enemies.

WATCH FOR

- commas
- abbreviations

TUESDAY **WEEK 35**

The saguaro is the tallest cactus. By the time it is 100 years old, it may be 5 meters (16 ft) tall. It has a smooth, waxy, fluted stem. it can store up to 200 gallons of water. The water heats ~~slow~~ slowly during the day, and the cactus stays cool. The water lets off the ~~heet~~ heat at night, and the cactus stays warm.

Error Summary

Capitalization	1
Language Usage	1
Punctuation:	
Comma	4
Period	2
Spelling	1

WEDNESDAY **WEEK 35**

A barrel cactus is shorter and ~~fat~~ fatter than some of the other cactuses. A full-grown one can be 1.5 meters (5 ft) tall and 60 centimeters (24 in) wide. It's stretchy, pleated sides let it store water. The barrel cactus gets larger. When it is full of water and smaller as the water is used up. the pulp can be used to make candy.

Error Summary

Capitalization	2
Language Usage	1
Punctuation:	
Apostrophe	1
Comma	1
Period	4

THURSDAY **WEEK 35**

Name ______________________________

The saguaro is the tallest cactus. By the time it is 100 years old, it may be 5 meters (16 ft) tall. It has a smooth waxy fluted stem. it can store up to 200 gallons of water. The water heats slow during the day and the cactus stays cool. The water lets off the heet at night and the cactus stays warm

WATCH FOR

- commas
- abbreviations

WEDNESDAY **WEEK 35**

A barrel cactus is shorter and fat than some of the other cactuses. A full-grown one can be 1.5 meters (5 ft) tall and 60 centimeters (24 in) wide. It's stretchy pleated sides let it store water. The barrel cactus gets larger. When it is full of water and smaller as the water is used up. the pulp can be used to make candy

WATCH FOR

- commas
- abbreviations

THURSDAY **WEEK 35**

Preview the 4 daily lessons to ensure you review or introduce skills that may be unfamiliar to students.

The Contest

groundhog day was a big day in the town where twins fran and fred lived. ~~Everywon~~ Everyone liked to watch phil the groundhog come out of his burrow. The TV station ran a contest. People had to guess the time phil would appear. The winners would be on the TV show Hello from Our Town, and they would also get a copy of the book, groundhogs forever.

Error Summary	
Capitalization	9
Punctuation:	
Comma	1
Period	2
Other	1
Spelling	1

MONDAY WEEK 36

Fran and fred read all about groundhog day. they learned that groundhogs come out of their holes on february 2nd. They help predict if there will be six more weeks of winter or if spring will arrive soon. If the groundhog sees his shadow, there will be more winter. If there is no shadow, winter will be ending soon.

Error Summary	
Capitalization	5
Punctuation:	
Period	2

TUESDAY WEEK 36

Name ______________________________

The Contest

groundhog day was a big day in the town where twins fran and fred lived. Everywon liked to watch phil the groundhog come out of his burrow. The TV station ran a contest. People had to guess the time phil would appear The winners would be on the TV show Hello from Our Town and they would also get a copy of the book, groundhogs forever

WATCH FOR

- titles of books and TV shows
- holidays

MONDAY **WEEK 36**

Fran and fred read all about groundhog day. they learned that groundhogs come out of their holes on february 2nd. They help predict if there will be six more weeks of winter or if spring will arrive soon. If the groundhog sees his shadow, there will be more winter If there is no shadow, winter will be ending soon

WATCH FOR

- holidays

TUESDAY **WEEK 36**

Fran and fred looked at old copies of North Country Magazine and found the times phil had appeared in past years. They decided Phil would come out at 235 pm. Fran entered their guess at 1014 am on january 30th. The station clerk told her to watch the groundhog day special on february 2nd to find out who had ~~winned~~ won

Error Summary

Capitalization	7
Language Usage	1
Punctuation:	
Period	4
Other	4

WEDNESDAY **WEEK 36**

The twins got up at 630 am on february 2nd. They thought about phil all day They watched the Groundhog Day Special at 500 pm. What a Surprise! At exactly 235 pm phil came out and saw his shadow. fran and fred had won! They would be on hello from our town and they would also get a copy of Groundhogs Forever.

Error Summary

Capitalization	9
Punctuation:	
Comma	2
Period	6
Other	5

THURSDAY **WEEK 36**

Name ______________________________

Fran and fred looked at old copies of North Country Magazine and found the times phil had appeared in past years. They decided Phil would come out at 235 pm. Fran entered their guess at 1014 am on january 30th. The station clerk told her to watch the groundhog day special on february 2nd to find out who had winned

WATCH FOR

- titles of magazines and TV shows
- colons in time

WEDNESDAY **WEEK 36**

The twins got up at 630 am on february 2nd. They thought about phil all day They watched the Groundhog Day Special at 500 pm. What a Surprise! At exactly 235 pm phil came out and saw his shadow. fran and fred had won! They would be on hello from our town and they would also get a copy of Groundhogs Forever.

WATCH FOR

- titles of books and TV shows
- colons in time

THURSDAY **WEEK 36**

Write about a person you know. Tell about something special that the person did. Tell about the person's childhood, teenage years, or adult life. Use words that tell what the person is like. Tell how the person's actions made a difference to other people.

FRIDAY – WEEK 1 **Biography: Walt Disney's Cartoon Magic**

Tell what you know about how the last three planets were found. Give their names and tell who found them. Write the dates when they were found. Use one of these topic sentences, or write your own:

- Uranus, Neptune, and Pluto are the last three planets to have been discovered.
- Curious scientists discovered the seventh, eighth, and ninth planets.

FRIDAY – WEEK 2 **Science Article: The Search for Planets**

Write a letter to Mrs. Faith Ringgold. Tell her what you like about her books and drawings. Tell the names of some of her books. Be sure to include your address, a closing, and your name. Use one of these closings, or one of your own:

- Very truly yours,
- Sincerely,
- Your fan,

FRIDAY – WEEK 3 **Letters: Letters to an Author**

Write what you know about salt. Tell where it comes from and how it is used. Explain why people need salt. Tell some interesting or unusual things abut salt. Use one of these topic sentences, or write your own:

- Salt is an important mineral.
- For ages, people all over the world have used salt.
- Did you know that salt has been used instead of money?

FRIDAY – WEEK 4 **Science Article: A Salty History**

Write what you know about barcodes. Be sure to tell what they look like, how they are read, and where they are used. Begin with one of these topic sentences, or write your own:

- Barcodes are a helpful invention.
- Barcodes are used in many ways.
- What do you know about barcodes?

FRIDAY – WEEK 5 **Science Article: Barcodes**

Describe the Grand Canyon or another place you know well. Tell where it is. Include words that tell what the place looks like. Put two adjectives next to each other in one sentence. Be sure to put a comma between them. Begin with a topic sentence like one of these, or write one of your own:

- The desert is a hot, dry place.
- There's a lot to see in the park.
- My neighborhood is an interesting place.

FRIDAY – WEEK 6 **Description: The Grand Canyon**

Write a summary of the news article about butterflies or the one about robins. Tell where and when the story takes place. Tell what happened and why. Begin with one of these topic sentences, or write your own:

- Something important happened in (Mexico, Virginia).
- There's good news from the (insect, bird) world today.
- Nature is putting on a good show in (Mexico, Virginia).

FRIDAY – WEEK 7 **News Articles: News on the Wing**

Choose one of these ideas and write a diary entry:

- Write an entry for June 10th. Tell what you did to get ready for the trip.
- Write an entry for July 1st. Tell what you did on the last day of your vacation at the beach.
- Write a diary entry about your own life. Tell about something that you did or how you felt about something.

FRIDAY – WEEK 8 **Journal Entries: Rosie's Diary**

Write a review of a book you like. Give the title of the book. Tell who wrote it. Give the names of the characters, and tell something about the story. Explain why you like the book, and say why you think others will like it.

FRIDAY – WEEK 9 **Book Reviews: Recommended Reading**

Write about one of the historic United States capital cities. Remember to capitalize the name of the city and state. Give some interesting facts about the city. Use a contraction in your paragraph. Begin with one of these topic sentences, or write your own. Fill in the name of the city.

- ____ is an interesting city.
- ____ is historic for many reasons.
- The city of _____ is full of history.

FRIDAY – WEEK 10 **Social Studies Article: Historic United States Capitals**

Write some more questions and answers for Wanda Know's interview with Bea Gone of the Travel Kids. Ms. Know might ask Bea about how the Travel Kids spent St. Patrick's Day, Columbus Day, Veterans Day, or Thanksgiving. Bea could tell about where the group went and what they did. Be sure to use capital letters for the names of holidays, months, places, and people.

FRIDAY – WEEK 11 **Interview: Kids on the Go**

Write the life story, or biography, of a famous person or of someone you know. Tell about things that happened during the person's life. Give information about the person's family, where the person lived, and any important dates in the person's life. Explain what made this person special. Be sure to use capital letters for people's names, and to use commas to separate numbers in dates and between the names of cities and states.

FRIDAY – WEEK 12 **Biography: John Glenn, Space Hero**

Describe Chief Seattle's friendship with the white settlers. Explain how he felt about the settlers, and why he felt that way. Tell about the ways he helped the settlers. Tell what the settlers did to honor Chief Seattle. Begin with one of these topic sentences, or write your own:

- Chief Seattle was a friend to the white settlers.
- The white settlers were lucky to know Chief Seattle.
- Chief Seattle helped the settlers in many ways.

FRIDAY – WEEK 13 **Social Studies Article: Chief Seattle and the Settlers**

When Shea got home, she told her family about what happened when she and Jigs went looking for the leprechaun. Write one or two paragraphs that tell what Shea said to her family and how they responded. Be sure to use quotation marks for the words spoken by Shea or other people.

FRIDAY – WEEK 14 **Fantasy: Shea and the Leprechaun**

Write what you know about walking sticks. Be sure to tell about how they look, how they grow, and what they eat. Begin with one of these topic sentences, or write your own:

- The longest insect on Earth is the walking stick.
- Have you ever seen an insect that looks just like a twig?
- Walking sticks actually have more in common with insects than with plants.

FRIDAY – WEEK 15 **Science Article: Undercover Bugs**

Use your imagination! Write another short story for the book The Adventures of Paul and Babe. Tell about something that Paul Bunyan and Babe the Blue Ox did. Explain how they made or changed something in nature. You might tell about how they made mountains, valleys, plains, or deserts. Tell when and where the adventure happened. Give the story a title.

FRIDAY – WEEK 16 **Fantasy: Short Tall Tales**

Write a story based on something from your own life. Tell what happened. Tell who was with you. You may want to change the real names to other names. Make up quotations to tell what people said. Use one of these ideas, or make up one of your own:

- Tell about something funny that happened.
- Tell about a time you learned a lesson.
- Tell about a gift you received.

FRIDAY – WEEK 17 **Realistic Fiction: Hand-Me-Downs**

Write directions for the safe use of your in-line skates. The directions can include how to buy skates and gear, how to skate for fitness, and how to fall safely. Explain the steps in order. Use sequence words in your directions. Begin with one of these topic sentences, or write your own:

- How can you use your in-line skates safely?
- Here are some suggestions for safe skating.
- Skating can be fun and safe, too.

FRIDAY – WEEK 18 **Instructions: How to Skate Safely**

"Meg's Prize" is a historical fiction story. It combines the real names of early TV shows and their theme songs with a story about a family's first TV set. Write your own historical fiction story. Tell about something that really happened. Add characters that you make up.

FRIDAY – WEEK 19 **Realistic Fiction: Meg's Prize**

Write a news story about a storm in your area. Tell when and where the storm took place. If there was rain or snow, tell how much fell. Explain what happened because of the storm. Use quotes from people that tell what they saw, did, or felt. Remember to keep to the facts. Don't add your own opinion.

FRIDAY – WEEK 20 **News Article: The Blizzard of 2003**

Write directions that tell how to make a sandwich, scrambled eggs, or something else you like to eat. Be sure to list the ingredients. Tell the amount of each ingredient needed, too. Give the steps for making the food in order. Use number sequence words like **first**, **second**, and **third**, or use other sequence words like **next**, **then**, and **after that**.

FRIDAY – WEEK 21 **Instructions: How to Make a Sand Sundae**

Write a review of a poetry book or another book you have read recently. Give the title of the book and the author's name. Be sure to underline the book's title. For a poetry book, describe a few of the poems and give their titles. Don't forget to use quotation marks around the titles of poems. For other books, describe their main focus. Tell what you like or don't like about the book. Tell readers why they should or should not read this book.

FRIDAY – WEEK 22 **Book Reviews: Poetry Book Reviews**

Tell what you know about the Boston Tea Party. Explain why the colonists were angry. Tell what they did about their problems. Tell how King George felt about the colonists' actions and how he treated them. Begin with one of these topic sentences, or write your own:

- A tax on tea caused a war.
- The Boston Tea Party showed how the colonists felt about King George's taxes.

FRIDAY – WEEK 23 **Social Studies Article: The Boston Tea Party**

Choose one of these ideas and write another letter:

- Write a letter from Anders to Tilly. Tell about the work Anders did on the trip from San Francisco to California.
- Write a letter from Tilly to Anders. Tell about Tilly's preparations for the trip to America.
- Write a letter from Anders to Tilly. Tell what Anders wants to do when the family reaches Portland, Oregon.

FRIDAY – WEEK 24 **Letters: Letters Home**

Think about "The Boy Who Cried Wolf," and then write one or two paragraphs about this fable. What lesson do you think the boy learned by the end of the story? How do you think he will act in the future? Do you think the villagers will ever trust him again? Be sure to give several reasons to support or explain your response.

FRIDAY – WEEK 25 **Fable: The Boy Who Cried Wolf**

Write one or two paragraphs that describe the Arctic tundra. Be sure to say where it is located, what the climate is like, and the types of plants and animals that live there. Start with one of these topic sentences, or write one of your own:

- The Arctic tundra is a cold, dry place.
- The animals of the Arctic tundra are adapted to the cold.
- Do you think plants and animals can live in a cold, frozen land?

FRIDAY – WEEK 26 **Science Article: Welcome to the Arctic Tundra**

Write a personal narrative like Liak's. Tell about your family. Describe the place where you live. Tell about some of the things you like to do. Begin with one of these topic sentences, or write your own:

- My name is ______.
- My life is very interesting.
- Let me introduce myself.

FRIDAY – WEEK 27 **Personal Narrative: Liak, an Inuit Girl**

Choose one of these ideas and write a personal narrative:

- Pretend you are Kendra. Write about the time that you did not do your homework.
- Pretend you are Kendra. Write about another adventure you had.
- Write about yourself. Tell about something that happened to you.

FRIDAY – WEEK 28 **Personal Narrative: The Dog Ate My Homework**

Choose one of these ideas and write a diary entry:

- Write an entry for January 2nd. Tell about the family celebration for the last night of Kwanzaa on January 1st.
- Write an entry for January 8th. Tell about the first day back at school after vacation.
- Write a diary entry about your own life. Tell about something that you did or how you felt about something.

FRIDAY – WEEK 29 **Journal Entries: A Holiday Diary**

Write what you know about robots. Be sure to tell what they do to help people. List two or more jobs they can do in one sentence. Begin with one of these topic sentences, or write your own:

- Robots are very helpful.
- If you need a job done, call a robot!
- Did you know that robots have been up in space and down deep in the ocean?

FRIDAY – WEEK 30 **Science Article: Who Ya Gonna Call? Robot Helpers!**

Write what you know about the history of calendars. Be sure to tell when they started. Name the groups of people who made early calendars. Tell a little bit about how calendars have changed, and which is used today. Use one of these topic sentences, or write your own:

- Since early times, people have tried to keep track of time.
- People have used the sun and the moon to make calendars.

FRIDAY – WEEK 31 **Social Studies Article: The History of Calendars**

Write a paragraph that summarizes information about shadows. Explain how they are made and how they change. Start your paragraph with one of these questions, or write your own:

- Have you ever seen shadows in the evening?
- Do you know what causes your shadow to look longer or shorter?
- What makes a shadow?

FRIDAY – WEEK 32 **Science Article: Shadows**

Tell what gravity is, and explain how it makes a roller coaster work. Describe the first hill on a roller coaster, and tell why it has to be the highest. Tell about the rest of the ride. Use one of these topic sentences, or write your own:

- Roller coasters need gravity.
- Without gravity, a roller coaster will not go.
- Gravity helps make roller coasters work.

FRIDAY – WEEK 33 **Science Article: The Ups and Downs of Roller Coasters**

A historical fiction story uses a real event to tell a story. A worker really did find a moth in a computer, and he called it a "computer bug." The log is displayed in the Smithsonian. Lt. Hopper really was on duty when the moth was found. Dan and Max are made-up characters. Write your own historical fiction story. Use a real event and made-up characters.

FRIDAY – WEEK 34 **Historical Fiction: The First Computer Bug**

Write what you know about cactuses. Be sure to tell about their size and about how the different types look. Describe the way the saguaro and barrel cactuses store water. Begin with one of these topic sentences, or write one of your own:

- The cactus is an unusual plant.
- Did you know that plants can grow in the desert?
- A cactus knows how to take the heat.

FRIDAY – WEEK 35 **Science Article: Cactus—A Desert Plant**

Think about "The Contest," and then write one or two paragraphs about this story. What was the contest about? What were the prizes? What did Fred and Fran do to try to win? How did they find out they had won? Be sure to give examples from the story to support or explain your response.

FRIDAY – WEEK 36 **Realistic Fiction: The Contest**

Language Handbook

Basic Rules for Writing and Editing

Contents

Capital Letters

A word that starts with a **capital letter** is special in some way.

Always use a **capital letter** to begin:

the first word of a sentence:	Today is the first day of school.
the first word of a quotation:	She said, "Today is the first day of school."
the salutation (greeting) and closing in a letter:	Dear Grandma, Thanks so much for the birthday gift! Love, Sherry
the names of days, months, and holidays:	The fourth Thursday in November is Thanksgiving.
people's first and last names, their initials, and their titles:	Mrs. Cruz and her son Felix were both seen by Dr. S. C. Lee. **Note:** Many titles can be abbreviated. Use these abbreviations only when you also use the person's name: **Mr.** a man **Mrs.** a married woman **Ms.** a woman **Dr.** a doctor **Capt.** a captain **Lt.** a lieutenant **Pres.** the president of a country or an organization
a word that is used as a name:	I went with Dad and Aunt Terry to visit Grandma. **Be Careful!** Do not use a capital letter at the beginning of a word when it is not used as someone's name: I went with my dad and my aunt to visit my grandma. **Hint:** If you can replace the word with a name, it needs a capital letter: I went with <u>Dad</u>. ⟶ I went with <u>Joe</u>.
the word that names yourself - **I**:	My family and I enjoy camping together.

the names of nationalities and languages:	Mexican, Cuban, and Nicaraguan people all speak Spanish.
the names of racial, ethnic, or cultural groups:	There were Asian, Native American, and African dancers at the festival.
the names of ships, planes, and space vehicles:	The president flew on Air Force One to see the USS Abraham Lincoln, a U.S. Navy aircraft carrier. **Note:** You must also underline the name of a ship, plane, or space vehicle: the space shuttle Columbia
to begin the names of these special places and things:	
• street names:	Palm Avenue, Cypress Street, Pine Boulevard
• cities, states, and countries:	Los Angeles, California, United States of America, Paris, France
• continents:	Asia, Europe, South America
• landforms and bodies of water:	Great Plains, San Francisco Bay, Great Salt Lake
• buildings, monuments, and public places:	the White House, the Statue of Liberty, Yellowstone National Park
• historic events:	The Gold Rush began in 1849. The Civil War ended in 1865.

titles of books, stories, poems, and magazines:	The story "The Friendly Fruit Bat" appeared in Ranger Rick magazine and in a science book called Flying Mammals. **Be Careful!** Do not use a capital letter at the beginning of a small word in a title, such as **a**, **an**, **at**, **for**, **in**, and **the**, unless it is the first word in the title. **Note:** When you write a title, remember . . . Some titles are underlined: **Book Titles:** Frog and Toad **Magazine Titles:** Ranger Rick **Movie Titles:** Bambi **TV Shows:** Sesame Street Some titles go inside quotation marks: **Story Titles:** "The Fox and the Crow" **Chapter Titles:** "In Which Piglet Meets a Heffalump" **Poem Titles:** "My Shadow" **Song Titles:** "Twinkle, Twinkle, Little Star"

Punctuation Marks

Punctuation gives information that helps you understand a sentence.

End Punctuation

Every sentence must end with one of these three punctuation marks: **. ! ?**

A **period** (**.**) shows that a sentence is:

giving information:	I love to read short stories.
giving a mild command:	Choose a short story to read aloud. **Note:** A period is also used in: • abbreviations of months and days: Jan. (January), Feb. (February), Mon. (Monday), etc. • abbreviations of measurements: ft. (foot/feet), in. (inch/inches), lb./lbs. (pound/pounds), oz. (ounce/ounces) • time: 8:00 a.m., 4:30 p.m., etc.

A **question mark** (**?**) shows that a sentence is:

asking a question:	Did you choose a story to read?

An **exclamation point** (**!**) shows that a sentence is:

expressing strong feelings:	Wow! That story is really long!

Comma

A **comma** (**,**) can help you know how to read things. Commas are often used in sentences. Sometimes commas are used with words or phrases.

Some commas are used to keep things separate. Use a **comma** to separate:

the name of a city from the name of a state:	El Paso, Texas
the name of a city from the name of a country:	London, England
the date from the year:	October 12, 2004
the salutation (greeting) from the body of a letter:	Dear Ms. Silver,
the closing in a letter from the signature:	Yours truly,
two adjectives that tell about the same noun:	Nico is a witty, smart boy. **Hint:** To see if you need a comma between two adjectives, use these two "tests": **1** Switch the order of the adjectives. If the sentence still makes sense, you must use a comma: **YES:** Nico is a witty, smart boy. → Nico is a smart, witty boy. **NO:** Nico has dark brown hair. → Nico has brown dark hair. **2** Put the word "and" between the two adjectives. If the sentence still makes sense, you must use a comma: **YES:** Nico is a witty, smart boy. → Nico is a witty and smart boy. **NO:** Nico has dark brown hair. → Nico has dark and brown hair.

Some commas help you know where to pause when you read a sentence. Use a **comma** to show a pause:

between three or more items in a list or series:	Nico won't eat beets, spinach, or shrimp.
after or before the name of a person that someone is talking to in a sentence:	**After:** Nico, I think that you need to eat more. **Before:** I think that you need to eat more, Nico. **Both:** I think, Nico, that you need to eat more.
between the words spoken by someone and the rest of the sentence:	Mrs. Flores said, "It's time to break the piñata now!" "I know," answered Maya.
after an exclamation at the beginning of a sentence:	Boy, that's a lot of candy!
after a short introductory phrase or clause that comes before the main idea:	After all that candy, nobody was hungry for cake.
before and after a word or phrase that renames or gives more information about the noun before it:	The cake, which had thick chocolate frosting, melted in the hot sun. Mrs. Lutz, our neighbor, gave Mom the recipe.
before the connecting word in a compound sentence:	The frosting was melted, but the cake was great. **Note:** A simple sentence always includes a subject and a verb, and it expresses a complete thought. A compound sentence joins two simple sentences together, so each of the two parts of a compound sentence has its own subject and verb. The two parts of a compound sentence are joined by a comma and a conjunction. The conjunctions **and**, **but**, **for**, **nor**, **or**, **so**, and **yet** are all used to join two simple sentences into one compound sentence. In a compound sentence, always place the comma before the connecting conjunction: Maya ate candy, **but** she was too full to eat cake. Nico ate candy, **and** he also ate a piece of cake. Nico is thin, **yet** he eats lots of sweets. Maya is chubby, **so** she watches what she eats.

Quotation Marks

Use **quotation marks** (“ ”):

before and after words that are spoken by someone:	“This was the best birthday party ever!” Maya said. **Note:** Punctuation that follows the speaker’s words goes inside the quotation marks: “May I have a piñata at my birthday party?” Martin asked. Mr. Flores replied, “You bet!” **Be Careful!** When the words that tell who is speaking come before the quotation, put the comma outside the quotation marks. When the words that tell who is speaking come after the quotation, put the comma inside the quotation marks: **Before:** Mrs. Flores asked, “Do you want a chocolate cake, too?” **After:** “I sure do,” said Martin.

Hyphen

Use a **hyphen** (-):

between numbers in a fraction:	One-half of the candies had walnuts, and one-quarter had almonds.

Apostrophe

An **apostrophe** (') helps show who owns something. You add an apostrophe after the name of an owner.

When there is just one owner, add an apostrophe first and then add an **s**:	cat + 's ⟶ cat's The cat's dish was empty.
When there is more than one owner, add an **s** first and then add an apostrophe:	cats + ' ⟶ cats' All the cats' cages at the shelter were nice and big. **Be Careful!** When the name of more than one owner does not end with an **s**, add an apostrophe first and then add an **s**: children + 's ⟶ children's The children'**s** cat was in the last cage. people + 's ⟶ people's Other people'**s** pets were making lots of noise.
Use an apostrophe when you put two words together to make one word. This is called a contraction. In a contraction, the apostrophe takes the place of the missing letter or letters:	I + am = I'm you + are = you're he + is = he's it + is = it's we + would = we'd they + will = they'll do + not = don't does + not = doesn't are + not = aren't could + not = couldn't have + not = haven't would + not = wouldn't

Plurals

A noun names a person, place, or thing. A **plural noun** names more than one person, place, or thing.

Add an **s** to make most nouns plural:	girl → girl + s → girl**s** river → river + s → river**s**
If the noun ends in **ch**, **s**, **sh**, or **x**, add **es**:	lunch → lunch + es → lunch**es** dress → dress + es → dress**es** brush → brush + es → brush**es** fox → fox + es → fox**es**
If the noun ends in **y**, change the y to **i** and add **es**:	fly → fli + es → fl**ies** story → stori + es → stor**ies** **Note:** If the noun ends in a vowel plus **y**, just add **s**: bay → bay + s → bay**s** key → key + s → key**s** boy → boy + s → boy**s** **Be Careful!** Some plural nouns do not have an **s** at all: child → **children** foot → **feet** man → **men** tooth → **teeth** woman → **women** goose → **geese**